Counselling in Male Infertility

DATE DUE

JE 2'03			
JE 2'03			

DEMCO 38-296

Counselling in Male Infertility

Sammy Lee
PhD, FIBMS, Dip Fert Couns

**Blackwell
Science**

Arnette Blackwell SA
  224, Boulevard Saint Germain
  75007 Paris, France

Blackwell Wissenschafts-Verlag GmbH
  Kurfürstendamm 57
  10707 Berlin, Germany

  Zehetnergasse 6
  A-1140 Wien
  Austria

First published 1996

Set in 10 on 12 pt Souvenir
by DP Photosetting, Aylesbury, Bucks
Printed and bound in Great Britain by
Hartnolls Ltd, Bodmin, Cornwall

The Blackwell Science logo is a
trade mark of Blackwell Science Ltd,
registered at the United Kingdom
Trade Marks Registry

DISTRIBUTORS

Marston Book Services Ltd
PO Box 269
Abingdon
Oxon OX14 4YN
(Orders: Tel: 01235 465500
         Fax: 01235 465555)

USA
Blackwell Science, Inc.
238 Main Street
Cambridge, MA 02142
(Orders: Tel: 800 215-1000
             617 876-7000
         Fax: 617 492-5263)

Canada
Copp Clark, Ltd
2775 Matheson Blvd East
Mississauga, Ontario
Canada, L4W 4P7
(Orders: Tel: 800 263-4374
             905 238-6074)

Australia
Blackwell Science Pty Ltd
54 University Street
Carlton, Victoria 3053
(Orders: Tel: 03 9347 0300
         Fax: 03 9349 3016)

A catalogue record for this title
is available from the British Library

ISBN 0–632–03906–X

Library of Congress
Cataloging-in-Publication Data
Lee, Sammy, Dr.
    Counselling in male infertility/Sammy
    Lee.. p. cm.
    Includes bibliographical references and
    index.
    ISBN 0–632–03906–X
    1. Infertility, Male—Patients—Counseling
    of. I. Title.
RC889.L366 1996
616.6'92—dc20   95-43041
                                       CIP

Contents

Foreword

Dr Lee's book deserves a wider readership than just those directly involved with counselling. For this is a book which raises and attempts to explain vital issues of masculinity and maleness, albeit within the limited context of male infertility, and it gets straight to the heart of the matter.

Dr Lee points out that male patients often develop serious depression and sexual impotence following a diagnosis of infertility. Once seen only as a woman's problem, it is now clear from research that, in around 50% of all cases of infertility, a male factor is involved. Infertility specialists and other health care professionals need to address this development and increase their knowledge and understanding of men's feelings in coping with this difficult situation.

Dr Lee describes clearly and without awkward technicality the techniques and advances in assisted reproduction for the practitioner, technician and scientist. He constantly reiterates the complex interaction of mind and body, and in the chapters on counselling techniques and theory, he returns to the important focus of masculinity.

He describes male infertility as one of society's taboo subjects, and draws upon current research and his own extensive counselling experience to stimulate debate and further research in male infertility.

Dr Lee wanted a lay reader, rather than a scientist or practitioner, to write the Foreword for this book, since its far reaching and introspective thoughtfulness about the nature of maleness takes is beyond the realm of being just a practitioner's handbook. He has cut a swathe through our reticence by addressing scientific questions which we can all approach intellectually, but which enable us to ponder much deeper matters.

Rex Cowan

Preface

Experts in male infertility in the UK may be counted on the fingers of a pair of hands, yet recognised infertility specialists number in the hundreds and are almost all gynaecologists (with a qualification of MRCOG or FRCOG in the UK or Board certified in the USA). A similar situation exists in the USA and throughout the Western world. What is it about male infertility that results in such isolation and desolation? Why are there so few experts and why the apparent lack of interest?

Here in the 1990s we are slowly becoming more enlightened; more attention is being paid to the male. Even with better understanding and clearer opportunities for diagnosis, it is interesting to observe that in spite of the availability of advanced sperm function testing, many specialists still pay little attention to this subspeciality. Reasons for this remain unknown. It is possible that because of our historical ignorance about male infertility, the *status quo* demands that we continue to ignore this aspect of infertility. Another possibility is that gynaecologists, being particular focused on women, are simply not very interested in men. Consequently, the male is an unknown quantity for these specialists.

My own experience in this area may throw some light on the matter. Men who have a low sperm count are often referred to me for further diagnosis. Frequently, these men have no count – 'low' being used as a euphemism. It seems, understandably so, that both male and female gynaecologists find it difficult to deal with infertile or subfertile men. When talking about male infertility, we are highlighting the difficulty in providing diagnosis as well as the problem of explaining to men that they have sperm dysfunction. Furthermore we are also dealing with a range of emotions in both the specialist and patient, since male infertility is one of the few remaining taboo subjects of the liberal Western world. With this in mind this book is written to help to bring about a more open understanding of male infertility. It is dedicated to specialists, patients and clients.

Sammy Lee
1996

Introduction

In the following chapters we shall explore possible answers to the questions raised in the Preface. We shall be looking at the plight of infertile men; exploring male ideology, female ideology, looking at how gender-based child development might affect male ideology and its role in determining how men behave in the environment of the infertility clinic. When looking at the issue of male and female ideology (particularly in Chapter 7), we are in controversial territory. Whether we accept the current conventional thinking in psychology that in general, most gender-specific differences lie in myth-making, or not, I feel that in this specialised field, the use of Shere Hite's (1991) description of male ideology is particularly relevant when dealing with male infertility. Perhaps one reason why Hite's description of male ideology is so relevant and accurate is the real possibility that, although there may be no quantifiable truth in such gender-specific stereotyping, many men actually or subconsciously believe in the myth of male ideology and the idea that they are 'mean and macho'. I have no doubt about the relevance of this in helping us to understand the differences (even if we only consider the ideologies as hypotheses) in men's and women's responses to infertility (Monach, 1993; Crawshaw, 1995). More about this is discussed in Chapter 7 itself.

Male ideology

Hite has described male ideology as an almost universal feature amongst men, whereby a patriarchal hierarchy has developed and dominated most cultures throughout the world's recorded history. The male ideology which she describes fits into the theme of this book, dovetailing neatly with all the ideas presented in this book regarding how men think about themselves and how these cherished beliefs are shattered by the stigma of male infertility. According to Hite, this ideology has come about by centuries of socially constructed behaviour and perceptions and not as a consequence of the 'natural' order of things as some would have it. It therefore has its roots in a social rather than a genetic basis and may therefore consequently be changed over a relatively short period of time.

Male ideology *continued*

Male ideology is all about male dominance in society. Under the ideology, men have a free rein over what roles they assume, so long as they are manly roles, i.e. hunter, breadwinner, head of the family etc. However, for men to adopt what are perceived as female roles or behaviour is taboo as men see this as inferior, i.e. men do not cry, they are not allowed to love nor display love as women do, they do not display their emotions in private and especially not in public. Male ideology in Hite's opinion dictates that men are men, which means that they are responsible, capable, brave, virile and macho, they do not need help; they are rational, logical, scientific and objective, but they are also afraid of their own emotions. By being emotionally distant, men seek to have power and control, which is a key part of men's value systems so that work, independence and dominance become all important. Thus men never let their guard down and always strive to keep control of all situations.

An examination of the background of treatment (Chapter 3) and aspects of the training of the doctors involved (in Chapter 10) may provide some further insights into the mysteries of male infertility and its failure to emerge from myth and mystery. By exploring the issue of man in crisis (Chapter 1) and looking at gender-roles, ideology (Chapter 7), culture and religion (Chapter 8), I am not so much setting myself up as an expert on how men's problems with infertility arise, rather I hope to stimulate debate and further research on the matter. I have not set out deliberately to be controversial, but in the process of researching and writing the book, many of the ideas seemed to make sense in helping to explain why men behave as they do in infertility clinics, in public, at work and in their homes, when they are faced with a diagnosis of male infertility. In a nutshell therefore, in these chapters I seek to provide some insight into why men have such difficulty in dealing with infertility.

In Chapter 1 we explore the issue of man in crisis. Here some 'armchair philosophy' regarding man in social crisis and the state of humanity is provided in order to stimulate debate and discussion on how modern society in the West seems to be heading towards a scenario whereby the fabric of its society may be drastically altered. Men who subscribe to the male ideology described by Hite (1991) and who have dominated society for centuries seem least well equipped to deal with the imminent changes. Women, whose female ideology has been subordinated to and by men in many societies throughout the world over several millennia, seem better equipped and prepared than their male counterparts for the changes ahead (see MacCormack & Strathern (eds.), 1980). In the main, part of the crisis may also be rooted in the way that Western women are adopting new roles. Throughout the 1980s, female empowerment has gained momentum; to such an extent that here in the 1990s, to some men, it almost seems as if they are on a roller coaster without brakes, heading unstoppably towards a destiny which threatens their existence (Greenstein, 1993). It seems as if all at once, Western women are now not only imitating some of the freedoms, ideas and roles of their non-Western counterparts (for example the sexual freedom of Tahitian women (Bloch & Bloch, 1980) or the relative equality of Kaulong women in New Britain (Goodale, 1980)), but also gaining new ground, for example, their choice to eschew traditional roles such as wife or mother, and by some taking up careers which had previously been accessible to men only (such as politics, banking, law, etc.). Moreover, leaving aside the idea of sexual politics, we live in an age when attitudes are changing. Indeed, there is a growing acceptance of single parent (mainly female) families, whilst more and more women are choosing to have children later in life or even to remain childless.

In many ways, this crisis seems to be mirrored by the growing awareness that male infertility seems also to be on the increase. It is ironic that as society (men and women) itself faces an imminent crisis, male infertility itself has contributed greatly towards infertility generally, becoming the thin end of a wedge which represents not just a reproduction revolution, but the beginnings of a social revolution which threatens to reduce sex to a pastime rather than a means of procreation (for further reading see Strathern, 1992).

Reading between the lines, many readers might indeed wonder whether the apparent increase in male infertility is a response to this crisis. Indeed falling sperm counts in men is a current hot topic and has been extensively debated in the pages of the *British Medical Journal* (Carlsen *et al.*, 1992; Bromwich *et al.*, 1994; Farrow, 1994; Irvine, 1994) and *The Lancet* (Sharp & Skakkebaek, 1993; Ginsberg *et al.*, 1994; Lee, 1994a; Editorial, 1995). Briefly, Carlsen *et al.* (1992) suggested that there was a general trend showing a global decline in sperm counts in men. Sharp & Skakkebaek (1993) proposed that environmental oestrogens might play a role in this apparent decline in sperm counts.

There were several other opinions expressed (Bromwich *et al.*, 1994; Lee, 1994a), essentially arguing that there was no real decline in sperm counts, and that the perceived decline might be explained away by methodological differences (Bromwich *et al.*, 1994) or by a general increasing interest in male infertility (Lee, 1994a).

It is important to note that decline in sperm count does not necessarily mean an increase in incidence of male infertility (see Chapter 2). Nevertheless, whether sperm counts are declining or not, none of the authors involved in the debate questioned the idea that there seems to be an increase in the global incidence of male infertility. Whilst it is possible that the ensuing crisis described in Chapter 1 might be a contributing factor to growing numbers of men with infertility, it is important to bear in mind that there is little unequivocal evidence that stress and anxiety cause infertility. Rather the main cause of declining fertility in men must be due to environmental factors. One possibility is water pollution (Ginsberg *et al.*, 1994). A report by the Danish Ministry of Environment (1995) clearly pointed the finger towards environmental hazards, such as oestrogens and chemicals; in particular pesticides which permeate both foods and water consumed by humans.

As mentioned earlier, manhood or masculinity are under attack, and whilst it is clear that environmental factors are strongly implicated, the power of the mind should not be underestimated. Aric Sigman, a psychologist who appears frequently in the media, feels that man is suffering from a feminist backlash (see also Greenstein, 1993). This possibility is discussed in the book. Whether feminist backlash or not, it seems certain that modern man is undergoing a collective type of crisis perhaps triggered by long-term unemployment, increasing female employment, and high rates of divorce as women begin to assert their independence. The final part of the jigsaw is perhaps the accelerating rate of suicides amongst 20 to 40 year old men (press release data from the Samaritans, 1994). When we explore this crisis no value-judgements are applied. The crisis may be perhaps viewed overall as mankind beginning to adjust, as traditional roles change, reflecting men's and women's ongoing state of maturation. The changes will almost certainly benefit mankind, but in the interim period, until man can adapt, some men will be in deep shock and crisis.

Whatever the effects of the crisis, these men will need support and with any luck will be able to undergo the transition to become fully functional males, able to assimilate and adapt to the new roles that will emerge in the future, but at present men seem to be struggling. Indeed, a documentary on BBC1 television in 1994, celebrating the International Year of the Family, titled *The Family Call: On Men*, showed that most family gender-roles follow traditional patterns and that modern man is still a myth. There are certainly more working women and they are indeed much more independent than their predecessors, but in the main working women also remain housewives for the time being (confirmed in an article in the *Daily Express*, 25 April 1995, by Kathryn Lister reporting on a study published by *Top Santé*, which found that among 5000 women interviewed, over 75% felt that their male partners still did not do their fair share of the housework, these women carrying out on average, twice the workload of their partners every day).

When Aric Sigman, a chartered psychologist and media person claims that man is suffering from a feminist backlash, he perhaps refers to a perceived rather than a real effect. Nevertheless, man's response to perceived threat is not to be underestimated.

With regard to the idea that we are going through a reproduction revolution (Lee, 1989), Morgan & Lee (1991) suggest three possible reasons for the reproduction revolution.

(1) They perceive that more couples are presenting with so-called primary infertility. This in itself represents a changing pattern in people's choices regarding family planning. Perhaps delayed childbirth, the pursuit of careers and chosen childlessness coupled with changing choices has given people far more options in life. In the 1960s and 1970s, women often chose to remain childless. However in the 1990s, the changing pattern of the family unit and increased liberation of women has led to women finding their reproductive horizons changing and extending, resulting in the possibility of abandoning a previous choice of childlessness. Hence the need for longer reproductive life and the apparent need for pregnancy in late reproductive life (witness the relative popularity of assisted reproduction techniques (ART) for post menopausal women).

(2) More couples are now coming forward for fertility treatment, which may indicate an increasing lack of babies for adoption. The widespread use of contraception, abortion and an increasing acceptance of single mothers may have also brought about changes in society. Thus heightened expectations may have led to reluctance, even refusal, to accept involuntary childlessness, which may be especially true of those with rising incomes.

(3) Medical advances and the role of the media are also factors. Soap operas rely on personalities, conflicts and sex. Infertility has all these. The media attention is voraciously consumed by the public. Morgan & Lee (1991) quote a study carried out by Stephen Harding, which showed that UK opinion was middle of the road for Europe. The study also showed that intrauterine insemination (IUI) and *in-vitro* fertilisation (IVF) are supported by about 85% of the public, but donor insemination (DI) only by about 50%. There is something about DI which disquiets the public.

Further incursions are made into some anthropological aspects of humankind. The role of religion, culture and beliefs are discussed in Chapter 8. The typical Western metropolis of today has a multiracial population and it is important to remember that differences in people's backgrounds may influence their behaviour, particularly in response to such stressful situations as infertility. We shall also look at how infertility clinics are geared for women and explore some of the ideas of feminist politics and IVF, with respect to the ways in which men either collude with or become victims of the system (Chapters 9 and 10). We shall also look at, in Chapter 7, the plight of men, particularly the neglected marginalised man, in infertility clinics.

Counselling in infertility is a highly specialised area. The Human

Fertilisation and Embryology Authority (HFEA) in the UK prescribes that support, implications and therapeutic counselling must be made available to all patients in licensed treatment centres. There are few other, if any, areas of counselling, which are given such credence and official recognition. This therefore places infertility counselling very much under the spotlight.

Counselling in general is a profession that seeks to provide its clients with an opportunity to deal with issues and problems in a safe and confidential environment. Through counselling, clients have an opportunity to address and resolve issues through the mobilisation of their own personal resources. By gaining new insight as a consequence of counselling, they may adjust their feelings, understanding and behaviour by decision making under their own control. Counselling is thus a relationship through which change and new understanding may be facilitated. Counsellors must therefore be competent, ethical and have a clear code of conduct. Competence encompasses having appropriate training, successful acquisition of skills, sufficient experience and regular supervision of practice. More about counselling is included in Chapter 6.

Counselling in male infertility is a subspeciality. Men may need counselling at any stage of their journey, whether it be at the first visit to the clinic, on diagnosis, during treatment, after failure of treatment, after treatment has ceased and in some cases years after treatment has ceased. The counselling required may relate to support, implications or therapeutic or all three at any one time. Counselling is counselling, whether it be for general issues or for those relating to infertility. Where some specialist knowledge of infertility and its treatments is useful to the counsellor in an infertility setting, so an understanding of men's peculiar traits (male ideology) and their unique responses to infertility may be similarly of value, when counselling men specifically. Crawshaw (1995) points out that people exhibit gender-specific reactions to fertility and parenting. She suggests that most women are preparing for motherhood from early on in life. Western society seems to reinforce the idea of maternity as a central female role in life. Men on the other hand do not seem to place such emphasis on fatherhood, which they see as just one of the roles available to them (Monach, 1993), although, ultimately, most men expect to become fathers. Indeed Monach has shown that men exhibit very different (gender-specific) reactions from women towards infertility. He suggests that female ideology allows women to express their feelings of sorrow about infertility and childlessness, whereas men are unable to allow themselves this 'luxury'.

Chapters 4, 5 and 6 deal respectively with how men feel when they are told that they are 'infertile', how we deal with such men and how we counsel them. When dealing with men, it is helpful to know the range of feelings that men experience. These feelings are outlined in Chapters 4 and 5. Apart from guilt and loss of self esteem, there seem to be issues concerning blame and punishment. These issues are key elements in counselling infertile men. Other key strategies involve looking at sources of support as well as exploring male ideology and issues of manhood with the client.

In Chapter 6, I have tried to bring together the key elements of Chapters 4 and 5. A model is also described which I have found useful in my own practice. In Chapter 6, further focus on counselling is provided in the case history of an 'idealised client' in conjunction with the model described therein. I feel it is important though to emphasise here that I do not see this book as a handbook on 'how to counsel men', but I hope that from these three chapters alone, anyone dealing with men in the infertility setting will immediately recognise some of the issues and problems that their clients bring and that the model and some of the suggested strategies will be of use when dealing with them.

Part of the problem concerning male infertility lies in the ongoing controversy over what constitutes a diagnosis of male infertility. The traditional method of assessing male fertility, the semen analysis (sperm counts) is of little value, hence the difficulty in advancing our knowledge and understanding. In Chapter 2 of this book we shall be looking at how establishing standards and a global test of sperm function may pave the way forward. Furthermore, male infertility is a challenge for the 1990s. During the 1980s, more and more specialists came to realise that male infertility accounts for up to 50% of all diagnoses of infertility. About 30% of all cases seem to involve male factors only, whilst 20% of cases include male infertility amongst other factors. Over the years, repro-duction technology has developed at breathtaking speed. However, unfortunately male infertility essentially remains in the dark ages, but things are beginning to change.

Since diagnosis of male infertility still relies on opinion which has been based little on fact, it means that a diagnosis of male infertility is shocking, not only because of the social stigma, but also because those who seek a second and third opinion find themselves becoming increasingly confused, isolated and frustrated. Problems are further exacerbated because the majority of societies in the world are male dominated. Indeed, most medical specialists, even in the field of obstetrics and gynaecology, are male (see Chapter 10). Moreover, infertility specialists are almost always gynaecologists. Perhaps, as a consequence of these factors, investigations and treatment of infertility have always been female oriented. Historically therefore, men have been able to deny involvement in infertility. Until very recently, little attention was paid with regard to the man in most infertility clinics (which even now are often held in gynaecology clinics in maternity buildings). As a consequence, men willing to acknowledge male infer-tility are only just beginning to stand up and be counted (see sections in

Chapter 4: How do men respond to male infertility? and Chapter 7: A modern male's outlook on infertility).

The domination of men in the speciality of gynaecology is discussed in Chapter 10, whilst there is a consideration of the legal, ethical and moral issues in Chapter 11. The legal framework provided by the HFEA is described briefly and compared with that in other countries. Also in Chapter 11, there is additional information on issues of concern. Here I have gone beyond the boundaries of my brief, since much of the details in this section centre on infertility as a whole. However, I feel that the issues bear consideration, because they mirror circumstances that have relevance to male infertility and indeed, men are usually involved in them, one way or another (as doctor or patient). Finally, the issue of informed consent is dealt with in this chapter. It is my opinion that we are still failing our patients on this matter.

From a counselling viewpoint (Chapter 6), as already mentioned, we shall be exploring the range of men's responses to diagnosis and to how we may begin to tackle the various issues that arise. This chapter is an attempt to provide a working model for dealing with men, whilst Chapter 12 is intended as a summary of the many interwoven subjects that go to making up this book.

I wish to make special mention of Chapters 2 and 3, which are rather medical in nature. I make no apologies for this. It is my personal opinion that because of the specialist nature of the field, any counsellor would be well advised to be highly informed. If the client feels that he (or she) knows more than you (and many are quite expert), the counsellor may lose credibility to such an extent that a working relationship may then no longer be possible. The early chapters therefore seek to provide basic knowledge on the stage of the art with respect to the medical aspects of male infertility, both diagnosis and treatment.

I hope you will find this book useful.

Acknowledgements

This book is dedicated to my long-suffering family; in particular my wife Karen, Joyce, my daughter and Jonathan, my son. Special mention should also be given to my Dad, William and my parents-in-law, Paddy and June Donaldson, 'Grandee' and 'Gran' for their support and encouragement.

I owe a great debt to my friend and mentor Sue Jennings. Finally, I would like to acknowledge the help and support from the following friends and colleagues: Himansu Basu, Roy Davies, Mike Duggan, John Erian, Ian Treharne and Jeremy Wright. I would also like to thank Lawrence Mascarenhas for ensuring I took regular breaks from writing and to Kathy Mabbett for doing the figures (Joyce did Fig. 4.1). Thanks must also go to Sarah-Kate Powell, Sue Moore, Teresa Heapy and Lisa Field for their help and professional support with the manuscript.

Finally, special mention is due to Argentum, located at the Royal Society of Medicine, 1 Wimpole Street, London, for their excellent photographic work.

Sammy Lee
Portland Hospital
1996

Chapter 1
Man in Crisis

Introduction

When initially researching the details of this book, I realised that male ideology plays a significant role in how men behave, particularly when their beliefs and lives are challenged by a diagnosis of male infertility (see Introduction for a definition of male ideology). As pointed out in the Introduction preceding this chapter, so-called New Man does not really exist. Furthermore, one of the changes in Western society that brought about the idea of New Man, the increasing independence of women, threatens to bring about major changes in our society as a whole. In a book edited by MacCormack and Strathern in 1980, Levi-Strauss and Ortner are quoted extensively as accepting the almost ubiquitous sub-ordination of women, a matter also acknowledged by Hite (1991).

Now after centuries of male domination in the Western world, certain changes are occurring. These changes are probably not yet very significant in real terms, particularly since New Man remains a myth (even male ideology itself is rooted in myth, more about this matter is included in Chapter 7), but as Strathern (1992) has pointed out, our images of the future are rooted in both the present and the past. Thus, as the balance of power begins to adjust slightly, men begin to feel that their dominance, which relies on, as well as perpetuating male ideology, is under attack.

When considering men it is interesting that infertility treatment, which is viewed with great suspicion by feminists (Corea, 1985; Pfeffer and Woollett, 1983; Scutt (ed.), 1990) may also be contributing to male discomfort. In the following chapters, particularly Chapters 4, 5, 7, 9 and 10, we will look at how IVF clinics actually diminish and marginalise men, which is paradoxical, since they are usually run by men (although they are intended for women). Moreover, it seems that infertility itself in addition to male infertility is posing major questions of men and their ideology during the last two decades of this century and millennium. Take for instance, donor insemination (DI). It was developed as a form of treatment for couples, where the man was infertile. However, because of the way our Western kinship model works, men are usually wary of DI. A further example of how DI is able to disquiet men is seen

1

from the furore over so-called Virgin Birth Syndrome (Silman, 1993), when the public became aware that women were seeking to procreate by means of DI, in the absence of a father. At first glance, the absence of a father might be seen as the major problem, but our kinship system (Strathern, 1993) works in such a way that a man can never be sure of his fatherhood (that he really sired the child unless a paternity test is done) and it is common enough in our society that men often walk away from their child(ren).

After much thought, I came to the conclusion that the greatest reason for moral outrage was fear; the fact that here were women who wished to become mothers without recourse to men at all, and we are not talking about sexual intercourse. Quite simply, I suspect that men were projecting into the future and fearfully seeing images of a world dominated by women, where men might become redundant or drones. Indeed, if enough sperm were banked, men might not be needed at all except when banks needed replenishing.

It would be easy to come away from the Introduction to this book with the view that I was suggesting that male infertility may be a manifestation of man in crisis and that this, along with the environmental factors was responsible for the apparent epidemic, or pandemic of infertility amongst men. This is not quite the case, rather, it is almost as if male infertility itself is also part of the cause of man in crisis (and perhaps each might spark the other off in a chain reaction).

Irrespective of the above issues, I would venture so far to suggest that man in crisis involves women, since, as Strathern (1980, 1992) points out so well, men and women irrespective of their societies do not function alone and that humanity consists of males and females constantly interacting in various domains. Thus in spite of Western culture's penchant for individuality and independence, when I say man is in crisis, I should really be saying 'humankind in crisis'. We should not suppose however that the crisis is equally dangerous to both male and female. As the Virgin Birth Syndrome (Silman, 1993) furore suggests, women may arrive at a much empowered state, whilst men may find themselves crippled unless they begin to adapt quickly.

The theme of crisis is also relevant to the issue of increasing dependence on assisted reproduction by both men and women. How, in itself, the technology seems to be feeding on and fulfilling new desires (Strathern, 1992), whereby, before the advent of technology, people would accept their plight and get on with their lives, or look for different solutions, such as adoption or fostering. These issues are inevitably linked to the changing attitudes of women, as they pursue independent careers. Indeed, many now make a choice to have their children later or even not to have children. This latter choice is cushioned by new technology. The possibility of ovum donation (not surrogacy) has opened up new avenues, where women past normal reproductive age may now become pregnant and deliver babies. This area also offers up new possibilities with regard to kinship, since in this scenario, it is the father who has the genetic 'rights' and for once not the mother; so, inevitably, technology changes things and begins to change the way we look at kinship in the West (see Strathern, 1992, 1993). Thus when looking at crisis and how it arises, we may begin to imagine why assisted reproduction has become so powerful in the minds of those who must have children. Moreover, we seem to live in an age when the importance of 'possessing' children seems to have become paramount. It is conceivable that the importance of children is also bound up in the crisis scenario.

The possibility that some infertile and or childless couples harbour a secret unquantifiable conscience of guilt for some unknown act of sin, also seems to lead us neatly into this chapter's title; the idea that man is in crisis, because, although man is in crisis, he inevitably draws woman with him and guilt of an unknown origin (do we have echoes here of original sin?) seems ideally bound in with the image of humanity in crisis. With the idea that man is in crisis (see Fig. 1.1), let us first consider some of the wider aspects of how the crisis may be rooted. Rites of passage, for example, rituals marking the movement of social status such as birth, puberty, marriage and having children, have an important role in life. These rites hold important places in society marking transitional stages in life (Bee & Mitchell, 1984; Jennings, 1995; Levinson, 1978; Mac-Cormack & Strathern (eds.), 1980). They could be considered to be like signposts, helping us to identify where we are and where we are going. Without them, we become lost. It is common for age roles to be connected with rites of passage. Often rituals involve visual signs of change, for example: wedding rings; certain African and South American tribes practise ritual mutilation (MacCormack & Strathern (eds.), 1980), the Samoans endure and display tattoos as a mark of manhood (many die in the process of being tattooed).

Modern life in the West has begun to lose many of these rituals. As technology replaces old ways, many traditions are lost in history. The intrusion of technology into the Third World seems to be bringing about a mirroring of this loss of rituals, albeit at a slower rate. In the West many age roles have now become blurred, so that entry to manhood or womanhood may occur at three possible ages 16, 18 or 21. This results in rites of passage losing much of their symbolic power, which means that we begin to lose our own images of ourselves in such a way that the future presents itself with uncertainty. Because, the future belongs to the present regarding how we imagine what might happen to us, as our images of the future become blurred we seem to lose our way, becoming displaced, since the roots on which society lies depend on the past, which helps us to make ideas of the present (Strathern, 1992). This feeling of displacement also occurs when men and women are told that

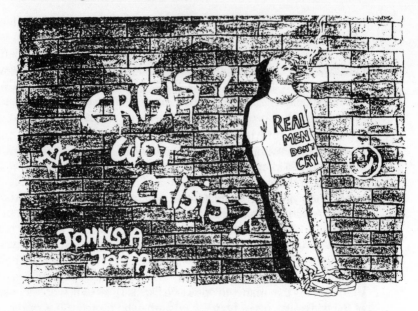

Figure 1.1 *Man in crisis?* This figure symbolises the state of debate on the issue of man in crisis. A crisis which may play a role in men apparently undergoing a decline in fertility, but also a crisis to which diagnosis of male infertility may make a substantial contribution. The changes in society reflected by the idea of man in crisis centre around growing female empowerment. Women are beginning to reassert their rights to be involved in matters unrelated to motherhood and the home. These changes in Western society are affecting men greatly. Within the arena of infertility, men seem to be similarly in crisis; although feminists feel that infertility clinics exploit women, men are managed equally harshly within the system existing in these modern 'temples of fertility'.

they are infertile, since the future becomes uncertain from that point on, because until then, most of them had never considered the possibility that they would not become parents.

Male and female taboos

Keeping with the theme of man in crisis, consider the following that menses, pregnancy and childbirth are also issues which affect men greatly today. In New Guinea, and other societies in Africa and the Pacific, men fear female vaginal blood – not only is it seen to be polluting, it is genuinely thought to weaken the man it touches (Gillison, 1980; Goodale, 1980).

It is interesting that so many Third World countries still have taboos about menses. In many of these cultures, the women must segregate themselves from the world of men for the duration of their bleeding. It is paradoxical, since the bleed is also recognised as a sign of fertility; men might therefore be jealous of women's ability to bear and deliver children, which is outside their own capabilities and so is particularly challenging to male belief in supremacy. For the Gimi people of Papua New Guinea, Gillison (1980) suggests that one possible reason for men's disgust concerning menstruation might be their fear of being symbolically devoured by women. Since this book is concerned with infertility, the case history below serves to demonstrate how men's preoccupation with the polluting nature of menstruation may lead involuntarily to infertility. It is also interesting to note how widespread in the world and not just in the third world, this idea of pollution is. The importance of the case history is relevant to any society: African, Pacific, Asian, etc., wherever sex is proscribed during menstruation.

Case history 1.1

Mr and Mrs D were consulting for long-term infertility of nine years duration. They had had some basic investigations which revealed no obvious problems in Mrs D and the borderline oligozoospermia (low count) in Mr D's semen sample. During the consultation it became very clear that Mr and Mrs D were orthodox Jews and were strict adherents to Judaic law, which does not allow for sex during the period of menstruation, and for the seven 'unclean' days following the cessation of bleeding, which would represent a 'defilement'. It turned out that part of Mr and Mrs D's problem lay in her very short cycle, which meant that the fertile period lay within the 'proscribed' part of her menstrual cycle.

As witnessed in Case History 1.1, in some cultures, the pregnant woman must even be avoided in terms of sex, hence perhaps one of the reasons for men to have a second and third wife. Indeed, even birth is something which men traditionally avoid. In the Western world, in recent years, men have been encouraged to attend the birth, which in other societies is taboo (Goodale, 1980), but this has recently been challenged by Michel Odent, a well known natural birther. He feels that perhaps modern man has been pushed too far in having to adjust to a fairer deal for woman and that it is okay for men who feel that they are happy to wait in the 'traditional prospective father's room' rather than attend the birth itself. Perhaps the process of birth itself is too traumatic for men, which again may be rooted in their fear and jealousy of women (Greenstein, 1993).

In many cultures, men are excluded from the act of childbirth (Mac-Cormack & Strathern (eds.), 1980), although in some cultures, such as Eskimo or Maori, the man has an intrinsic role and performs a number of rituals with regard to the birth. However, perhaps as a consequence of the feminist movement, men in the Western world are now encouraged to play an active role; however it seems that, because in the West, they have no clear rituals to enact, the process is not as emotionally rewarding as it might be. Post partum, up to 25% of men who are adversely affected report a type of depression (Heggenhougen, 1980). They suffer from a syndrome involving feeling run down, feeling low-down and weakness. Many symptoms quoted are similar to those of pregnancy. Is it an adverse reaction which equates to competition? Furthermore, the symptoms seem to tie in well with the myths and superstitions of societies in the Pacific (Gillison, 1980; Goodale, 1980), who feel that women, sex and menstruation in particular are sufficiently polluting that they cause weakness and even death itself. It is therefore possible that those men affected by attending the birth of their child are participating in an act which subconsciously challenges them, perhaps inducing a state of 'envy' or awe, with which they are unable to cope, thereby leaving them in a state of crisis.

Even today, within the Jewish religion a woman must remain segregated during the menses and sex is not allowed during this time (see Case History 1.1). Even in the Western world, sex during the time of menses remains a great taboo. The bleed is considered shameful and 'dirty'. These issues may affect men strongly. The link with birth is a strong one and may have underlying effects on men and their ideas of fatherhood.

Roles in society

Roles play an important part in how people identify themselves (Levinson, 1978). Social systems rely on interlocking positions. Age roles have already been mentioned earlier, in the introduction of this chapter. Transition marks the point at which a person enters a new age role, which often involves a rite of passage (initiation), for example, birth, coming of age, marriage and death (Jennings, 1995; MacCormack & Strathern (eds.), 1980). Role strains occur as people move from one role to the next (Levinson, 1978). Clearly, during transitional periods, the roles a person adopts become unstable, until the individual is able to establish a new life structure. For some it takes longer than others. There is an analogy here, if we look at society as undergoing transition in its many roles, perhaps as society matures, roles too may become unstable.

Perhaps we may see a link between mankind in crisis and the idea that society (both male and female) is going through a transition phase, and that roles and rituals have unequivocally become altered or blurred and that many roles and rituals are becoming to all extent and purpose, lost. Take for instance sex roles, on which further discussion will be found in Chapter 7; here is a suitable point to explore some aspects of the change going on in this particular sphere. The current debate over sex role differences questions how they arise; nature or nurture? Why are men and women different? Sex roles in childhood are still much as they have been, but in adulthood sex roles are becoming blurred, hence perhaps the attack on the male psyche. Indeed in terms of the depression syndrome that some men feel after attending childbirth (discussed earlier in this chapter), the act of parenthood taken up by a man who has observed birth seems to raise the stock of his mate in such a way that he seems challenged. Perhaps for some men this is a point where female equality is subconsciously established. For some men the idea perhaps of a woman's achieving equality through motherhood is too much, hence the ambivalence and resulting male infertility (refer to section on ambivalence in Chapter 5).

Traditional sex roles had a validity in the past; today as mankind undergoes transition, new sex roles are coming into existence, but as was pointed out earlier, these areas are as yet unstable and still being redefined. It is likely that the old sex roles limited human potential, since sex-oriented behaviour of the type that existed, clearly gave males more power, status and desirability than might be warranted. This has certainly been reinforced by the mass media in modern times, which have as a consequence enhanced male superiority and female passivity even more. These notions may now be beginning to come to an end.

Males must therefore begin to adapt. As mentioned earlier in the chapter, male infertility may in part be due to these emergent changes; there has been much debate in recent years (1992–5) on the notion that sperm counts in man are falling globally. All sorts of excuses have been given ranging from the aftermath of the Chernobyl nuclear accident to environmental pollution. However, there is a possibility that the environmental causes of declining male fertility may not be the only factors involved. What if in fact the issue of man in crisis was also affecting fertility in some men? Imagine too, the crisis and turmoil as men with a diagnosis of infertility are unable to deal with the idea of it. The state of crisis, for man as a whole, and for infertile men, is likely to persist until perhaps androgyny (the incorporation of the male and female attributes in one person) becomes the accepted norm. Then individuals will be able to express the feelings and emotions of either sex without being under threat. Some, perhaps many, of today's men might not be able to survive this change (Greenstein, 1993).

Family roles too are changing rapidly. There are increasingly more divorces, and the number of single parent families is increasing at an exploding rate. Previously there was a clearer life cycle. For example, take the following progression (Bee & Mitchell, 1984): newly married with no children, then married with first child approaching, married with children encompassing the new role of parenthood (and children adopting the role of childhood with adults adjusting to role of bringing up children), married with children grown up, married with children having left home (once again a shift in role), then married and own children married (resulting loss of role of parenthood), married with one's own married children having children (now adopting the role of grand-parents). These roles now begin to change as we, the human race, are in transition and the above roles have altered and become unstable. Untraditional family forms have begun to enter the picture, for instance, single parents living with children, gay/lesbian households and divorced parents marrying to form households with siblings of diverse back-grounds under one roof.

Family life has become very fragmented and our Western way of looking at kinship has begun to change; indeed technology is further helping to accelerate things. In the past kinship was a symbol of immutability (Strathern, 1992), but artificial means of procreation require new thinking of our kinship model, so much so that a founda-tion of human existence has now changed sufficiently that we no longer have as clear a reference point on which to base our relation-ship with others.

Even within families expressing traditional roles, there is often now the additional strain of the mother working. Despite many advances in Western society, women still are taking on too many roles, since most men have yet to undertake their own fair share of domestic duties. This leads to strain for the female partner and is one reason for marital conflicts.

Among single parents depression is common. If these family situa-tions have come into existence as a consequence of divorce, it is likely to leave long-lasting scars and may also be linked to behavioural difficulties in the children, if any. Furthermore, even where two divorced families are blended there is a need for readjustment of roles all round. In work roles too, men feel particularly under attack. These roles occupy most of our lives. Most people define themselves, in the West, according to their work (Bee & Mitchell, 1984). It fills a social and psychological need (in addition to subsistence needs). Role integration is necessary for good mental health. A person may have many roles, but in good health, roles emerge which have more priority and roles recede in their importance at different times. In role strain, too many roles emerge in importance at one time. Conversely, when there are too few important roles, role strain may occur, e.g. among 'supermums', or those men who feel that their life roles have diminished, e.g. unemployment, feminist backlash or whatever.

Rituals, birth and rebirth

Rituals are often used to mark transition points as a person passes from one role to another. Interestingly, the idea of rebirth is a strong one with respect to rituals. In Australia, aboriginal boys undergo a ritual at puberty involving a re-enactment of death and rebirth in order to emerge into life as adults. Similar symbolic death and rebirth initiation rites are followed by Thoma society initiates from the Sherbro people of Sierra Leone (MacCormack, 1980b). Rituals elsewhere such as initiation (bar mitzvah, coming of age, etc.), marriage and funeral rites, mark a movement from one phase of life to another, thereby helping those left behind to adjust to the change that a member of the community has undergone.

In many religions and societies, the idea of death is strongly linked with the idea of rebirth (Jennings, 1995). Life is full of such symbolism. In some ways, the life cycle of birth, death and rebirth (symbolically life after death) is therefore re-enacted in many of such rituals. The importance of life cycles is deeply rooted in man's past (MacCormack & Strathern (eds.), 1980), but in modern Western thought is no longer relevant. The adoption of a linear way of looking at life rather than a circular one may also contribute to the crisis that we are talking about; in the way that the future belongs to the present because of what we imagine might happen to us (Strathern, 1992), once we break with the idea of a life cycle, the future becomes much less certain and unpredictable.

For some men childbirth itself represents a significant rite of passage, marking a movement for themselves from the macho male type of life, to parenthood. Parenthood means responsibility, a relinquishment of a way of life which is in the Western world implanted into the male psyche from birth. Thus parenthood marks the death of a previous type of existence. This loss of freedom brought about by rebirth into the state of parenthood, a giving up of the macho life and the assumption of responsibility represents one of the strongest issues that relates to male ambivalence about parenthood. On the one hand is the unquantifiable drive and desire to father children, which neither experience of life nor role models seem yet to disillusion us about, whilst on the other hand is the potential fear of loss of freedom and the potential restrictions of fatherhood and responsibilities. The prospect of parenthood or the reality of becoming a parent may therefore challenge men to such an extent that they abandon the child(ren) in an act of denial or they may find themselves unable to function properly and in a state of crisis. This ambivalence may also explain why some men in infertility clinics are not as keen as their partners in pursuing treatment (see Case History 1.2).

Case History 1.2

Mr and Mrs F attended for counselling with regard to concerns about treatment. They were unsure whether to proceed with treatment or to call it a day. A contract for four sessions was made. Initially, it seemed a simple enough case. Here was a couple who just wanted to explore their options. At first, Mrs F made most of the running and it seemed that the doubt lay in her mind. She simply did not know whether or not she should consider any more IVF attempts. At this point Mr F was apparently keen to proceed. A number of side issues were also dealt with during subsequent counselling sessions. In the third session, as Mrs F became more positive about IVF, suddenly Mr F became unsure. It seemed that once faced with the reality of further treatment, in a way, his bluff had been called. The final session was taken up with his issue of ambivalence. In fact he feared what parenthood would mean, to him, to his relationship with Mrs F, and to his life style. He was most worried about his career, which he thought would stagnate because his perceived immobility as fatherhood meant 'taking roots'. In a way, Mr F wanted to be like Peter Pan and to continue to enjoy a life of freedom, which he felt fatherhood would take away.

The gradual erosion of our rites, rituals and symbols therefore has left us grabbing at various straws. There are few constancies in society today. As described previously, the age of majority has become so clouded, and indeed, although the legal age at which a person may have sex is 16, it is common knowledge that many indulge in sex as early as 13. Interestingly, the newspapers and television give us many clues about one of the Western world's last icons; that of the cult of children. The need for couples to buy what they may see as absolution, by paying for infertility treatment (in a way like the buying of indulgences – payments formerly made to the church to avoid time in purgatory prior to Judgement Day – the more you paid, the more hundreds of thousands of years you were let off) in order to have children, has also created a new scenario, rendering clinics as modern homes of a cult that has existed since the beginning of time (MacCormack, 1980b; Gillison, 1980; Goodale, 1980), that of fertility. The high priests and priestesses of this modern fertility cult are the personnel of infertility clinics. Extraordinarily, in a strange and fascinating way, the modern Western way of viewing fertility has therefore itself become reborn today as a type of religion. It is interesting to note that fertility goddesses are a part of the world's natural heritage and mythology. Seemingly, we have gone full circle. This new cult of fertility differs greatly from older cults insofar as the fertility worshipped today is of a new breed, that of one involving modern technology and reproduction without sex. In her book, *Reproducing the Future*, Strathern (1992) points out that when societies reproduce ideas, the copies are never exact, often resulting in a

Case History 1.3

Mr I was a fifty year old man who after many years of infertility had asked for counselling. At 40, he had been informed that his sperm count was low. This had been a great shock to him. At the time, he had been a successful person and was a middle manager with London Transport. Within three years of the diagnosis, his health had deteriorated and he had a stroke. At the time of counselling, he had still been unable to work and had been given an early pension. He was depressed and still had not come to terms with his infertility. Mr I is an ideal example of a man plunged into crisis by a diagnosis of male infertility.

Conclusion

Man is currently living in a time when women are redressing several millennia of subjugation. As women begin to redress the balance, man is suffering from role strain. Some of his traditional roles and the rituals that used to belong to him are changing as a consequence of female empowerment, but some of the changes are occurring because mankind as a whole is growing and developing. Whatever the reasons, life and society are changing rapidly. In the years to come we may see many things which will challenge our traditional values and beliefs, which we will find odd and will provoke much controversy and debate; take, for instance, the virgin women and/or lesbian couples who attend DI clinics for children without sex (Silman, 1993). Will we also see, in the future, gay male couples seeking women willing to provide them with surrogate pregnancies (possibly with donor eggs?). Will men be willing to risk male pregnancy? Would this equalise the sex roles?

Man in crisis is not necessarily a bad thing. In the long run, it may lead to a better society. In the interim, man is very much under the cosh. One of the ways the crisis may manifest itself is by reducing the fertility of some men, which may account for part of the growing numbers of men with a diagnosis of male infertility. The other reason for a growing epidemic of male infertility probably lies in the phenomenon of declining sperm counts observed since about 1970 (probably caused by a number of environmental factors, such as pesticides or artificial oestrogens). Because of the severe problems that a diagnosis of male infertility generates we may therefore also be on the threshold of an epidemic of men in a state of psychological crisis and resulting depression.

The wider scope is beyond the compass of this book, but in relation to male infertility we need to take into account that the crisis may be contributing to men's problems and to make it easier for such men to stand up and be counted and to reduce the stigma that surrounds it. We

also need to find ways to deal with the additional pressures that male
infertility itself superimposes over the 'crisis' and to provide access to
counselling and to promote participation in group and support work. A
lot of work and education must yet be done.

Chapter 2
Diagnosing Male Infertility

Introduction

A diagnosis of male infertility is a severe blow to a man. In the light of this, one might imagine that the basis on which such a diagnosis might be made and given should be both precise and accurate. Regrettably, this is not necessarily the case. In the Introduction I have alluded to the fact that much needs to be done both in terms of basic research and in the use of improved methods for determining sperm function or dysfunction. It is also my belief that once we have achieved the above aims, we shall also be in a better position to improve on our treatment outcome success rates, which even now rarely exceed 5% live birth rates in any treatment (for male infertility).

For those wanting more detailed information on male infertility, see the following: Glover *et al*. (1990), Hull (1991), Jequier (1986), Jequier & Crich (1986), Lee (1991a,b,c; 1994c), Jennings & Lee (1995) and Rajfer (1990).

Traditional methods of diagnosis

Traditionally, when trying to obtain a diagnosis regarding male infertility, specialists still rely on semen analysis, which in most hospitals in the UK, USA, Europe and throughout most of the world (see the manual published by the World Health Organisation on the subject) means a simple count of the sperm numbers in the ejaculate. Semen analysis involves assessing a sample of the semen in specially designed counting chambers such as a Makler, a Neubauer or a Horwell. By placing a small known volume (20–50 µl) of the semen sample into a counting chamber, a sperm count, motility and percentage abnormality may be estimated (see Fig. 2.1).

Sperm count is usually scored as so many millions of sperm per millilitre of fluid. In some hospitals a cursory subjective figure for percentage motility is also given (in other words, a hundred sperm will be examined, and the number that move and the number that do not, are scored; the total number of motile sperm out of the hundred gives us the percentage motility). Thus if 55 of the 100 sperm are motile, the

15

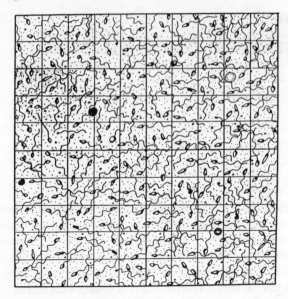

Figure 2.1 *Grid on a counting chamber.* This shows a typical grid. These types of grids have been used in semen counting chambers for years as methods of providing sperm counts. The number of sperms in a large grid, as shown in the Figure (5 × 5), usually represents so many millions of sperms per ml of semen (about 70 million per ml in this case).

motility will be 55%. More recently, some of the better laboratories also give an analysis of the percentage abnormality rate (for abnormality, the same count is done as for motility, except that a count of the normal and abnormal looking sperm is made instead, thereby allowing us to calculate the percentage abnormality rate), as well as subjectively analysing the quality of sperm movement, which is described as progression. This parameter takes into account how strongly and purposefully the sperm move. Usually progression is scored on an arbitrary scale ranging from one to a maximum of four. One out of four is very poor, failure of fertilisation would be quite likely if we used such a sample for IVF. Two out of four is sub-optimal. Three out of four is normal (most donor samples score three or better). Four out of four is excellent and is only seen in donor samples (in my own experience).

Definitions of male infertility

From semen analysis, in the past and even today, diagnoses of male infertility have been made in the following way: a poor count, a condition described as oligozoospermia, means that there are fewer than 20 million per ml in the sample. In cases of asthenozoospermia, the count may be normal, but the motility is below 40%. In cases of teratozoospermia, the count and motility may be normal, but the sample might reveal a high abnormality rate (more than 60%). Combinations of the above are also possible, such as oligoasthenozoospermia (low count and low motility), oligoasthenoteratozoospermia (low count, low motility and high abnormality rate); the most severe infertility short of azoospermia (which is the official word to describe a sample with no sperm in it at all). It is important to bear in mind that neither oligozoospermia nor asthenozoospermia alone indicates sperm dysfunction (Irvine, 1992; Jennings & Lee, 1995).

Semen analysis is useful as a first port of call, because it immediately tells us whether sperm are present or not. About 5–10% of all male infertility is attributable to azoospermia (causes for this condition are discussed later in this chapter). It is also useful if both a low count and low motility has been diagnosed; for example oligoasthenozoospermia. In these situations the motile sperm count must be less than 8 million per millilitre, by definition (motile sperm count = count multiplied by motility). So although semen analysis on its own is not a reliable method of detecting all male infertility, it is a good place to start, because it will identify the worst problems. Moreover, the analysis will also tell us whether the patient is able to ejaculate or not.

Factors affecting semen quality

Semen parameters are also known to vary widely from day to day, month to month and year to year, for a variety of reasons (duration of abstinence, bouts of illness, intake of alcohol, nicotine and caffeine), not least because it takes 60–70 days for a mature sperm to be made in the testis. It is important therefore to obtain at least three samples for analysis, before arriving at a complete diagnosis (for more information on spermatogenesis and spermiogenesis refer to Jequier & Crich (1986)). The effect of alcohol, smoking and caffeine intake on fertility is unclear, although there have been a number of studies published about such subjects in recent years. The current state of knowledge still suggests an absence of consensus. For my part, and I freely acknowledge the absence of properly controlled experimental data or studies, I am of the opinion that alcohol, smoking and caffeine may reduce fertility.

Humans have a huge range of variation, which is our great strength in terms of global dominance and survival, but this means that prospective controlled randomised studies are difficult to set up. It also makes the interpretation of data from such studies difficult. Nevertheless, after working as a specialist in male infertility for over five years now (and experience of over 1000 patients, with data on file) I have come to the conclusion that, if a man has a high sperm count and good percentage motility with demonstrable sperm function (for example, they prepare well or perform well in mucus or achieve a high fertilisation rate in IVF), then alcohol intake, smoking or caffeine intake must be extremely excessive before we would expect a deleterious effect on sperm quality. However, if a man has a borderline or sub-optimal semen analysis, then the above factors may contribute strongly to subfertility.

The effect of smoking (nicotine) is likely to act physiologically and pharmacologically at the hypothalamic level. The hypothalamus (an area of the brain) is a major control centre and is often described as the conductor of the orchestra (the orchestra being the many endocrine glands in the body, such as the pituitary, adrenals, thyroid, etc.). Interestingly, the hypothalamus is also highly responsive to emotions and stress in particular, as well as being highly responsive to nicotine. Alcohol may have an effect on the hypothalamus, but in terms of subfertility is more likely to be having a direct action at the testicular level. The testes are reproductive organs in the body, which on a minute-to-minute basis are actively involved in mitosis and meiosis (cell division). Sperm start their life as round cells called spermatogonia. These undergo mitosis (normal cell division) until they begin meiosis (cell division which only reproductive cells such as sperm and ova undergo, resulting in each cell having only 23 chromosomes instead of the normal 46).

The first stage of meiosis involves primary spermatocytes and secondary spermatocytes. The secondary spermatocytes must still undergo a final process during which they pass through a stage when they become as spermatids (early spermatids are still round cells and it is only during the final period as a spermatid that the characteristic 'tadpole' shape of adult sperm becomes apparent. From spermatogonia to mature sperm takes 60–70 days. Because the testes contain sperm at all these intermediate stages, as well as many millions of adult ones, at any one time, we might imagine that alcohol intake would be likely to have a direct effect on spermatogenesis. Alcohol is a poison. Even at very dilute concentrations, alcohol may be shown to slow down cell division and growth on cells grown in culture in the laboratory. It will also kill some cells. It is reasonable to postulate that alcohol may also slow down cell division and growth of sperm cells in the testes. If this is so, one day after an alcoholic binge, we might expect a man to have lower motility than otherwise. Furthermore, two months after the binge we might expect a lowered semen count too. This is obviously a very simplistic way of looking at the possible problems of alcohol intake, but serves to provide some rationale which hopefully also makes sense to the patient.

As I mentioned before, few controlled studies are available. For illustrative purposes only (rather than proof) I provide the following three case histories which I hope will serve to demonstrate how cessation of alcohol intake or smoking may have a beneficial effect on the outcome of semen analysis (and in some cases on sperm function).

I have particularly chosen these three case histories, because some-

Case history 2.1

Mr F smoked heavily. In my experience this is revealed by severe teratozoospermia, sluggish sperm movement, the presence of debris in the semen and the presence of up to 5 million per ml germ cells (round immature sperm cells). One attempt at IVF resulted in failed fertilisation, despite more than five ova being recovered. Advice given following the IVF attempt centred on the cessation of smoking. At this time semen analysis routinely revealed a count in the 30s (million per ml), motility between 40–50%, poor progression of 1 to 2 and an abnormality rate constantly in excess of 90%. Additionally, germ cell count was always between 3–5 million per ml.

As Mr F began to attend to his smoking addiction, follow ups at three-monthly intervals proved fruitful. Slowly the abnormality rate improved. Finally, after 12 months, the semen analysis was now routinely giving the following parameters, count remaining in the high 30s, motility still 40–50%, but progression was now between two to three and the abnormality rate had dropped to about 70%. The germ cell count was also now below 3 million per ml.

The next IVF attempt produced fertilisation and subsequently a baby boy.

Case history 2.2

Mr X drank heavily. His semen analysis was normal, except that the abnormality rate was 99%. There were also (as is routinely the case when dealing with high alcohol intake) routinely more than 20 million per ml germ cells present in the semen. Mr X was denied IVF by a number of clinics and was told that he would never have children and must consider donor insemination (DI) as the only real option available. Mr X duly signed up for DI treatment with his partner. Whilst waiting for this treatment, Mr X also agreed to undertake the regimen of abstention.

After three months, the abnormality rate had fallen to 80% and the germ cell count to 15 million per ml. At nine months, the abnormality rate continued to be about 70–80%, whilst the germ cell count had further improved to between 5 and 10 million per ml.

Mr X's case is still being followed up. At around six months a spontaneous pregnancy was achieved, but this sadly spontaneously aborted at about ten weeks. Mr X may soon be starting DI treatment with his partner.

> **Case history 2.3**
>
> Mr N smoked and drank heavily. His count and motility were normal, and like Mr X and F, his abnormality rate was high (90%) and germ cell count was in excess of 20 million per ml. As before, follow up continued for 12 months, whilst Mr N gave up smoking and drinking alcohol.
>
> As with case histories 2.1 and 2.2, at three and six months, the abnormality rate and germ cell count improved. By nine months, the abnormality rate was down to 70% and the germ cell count down to about 10 million per ml.
>
> Within three months, Mr and Mrs N succeeded in establishing a pregnancy which delivered, following intrauterine insemination treatment.

thing positive came out from the follow ups. Of course success is not the norm in this field. To provide some data for comparison, over the years, I have only been successful in persuading 12 men to take up the 'regimen', of whom the above three are drawn from. The remaining nine did not produce pregnancies, but all showed similar substantial improvements and indeed, beyond 12 months, all were lost to follow up.

How do we assess sperm function (male infertility)?

One way to consider function is to look at the natural environment. Sperm are normally deposited at the cervix in hundreds of millions. The sperm that arrive at the ampulla, the site of fertilisation, have undergone an epic journey through the cervical mucus, across the uterus and through the Fallopian tube. The few thousand sperm that arrive at the ampulla may be considered as being an elite sub-group of sperm (the 'crack troops', or elite sperm), the roughest toughest sperm (Lee, 1991a,b,c). The poorer sperm, whether they be abnormally shaped or less motile, are lost mainly in the cervix and in the journey up the female reproductive tract. It is important to consider therefore that even in a fertile man there is possibly only a finite number of fertile (viable) sperm per ejaculate (perhaps just 1000 per 100 million). Therefore a man with severely reduced count, simply by looking at the mathematics, will have fewer elite sperm present in an ejaculate. The sperm that are capable of reaching the ampulla therefore demonstrate function, whilst those that get screened out at the cervix demonstrate dysfunction.

Since diagnosis is traditionally limited to semen analysis, which in matter of fact usually tells us little about sperm function (Erian & Lee, 1990; Bromwich *et al.*, 1994; Irvine, 1992, 1994; Lee, 1994a,c; Jennings & Lee, 1995), this explains some of the problems in research in this field. Semen analysis may be inaccurate in diagnosis, because 5–10% of men with normal semen analysis will fail to fertilise ova during IVF, whilst 25–40% of men with just oligozoospermia or asthenozoospermia will demonstrate the ability to fertilise ova during IVF. Therefore, studies attempting to assess treatments of male infertility using semen analysis as a diagnostic assessment method have been basically flawed. As there is no globally accepted method of diagnosing male infertility, no one is using the same yardstick when doing research. Therefore we are not in a position to compare like with like. This means that opinions on male infertility vary enormously. In a way, IVF could be argued as being the ultimate test of sperm function.

Certainly, IVF points us in a certain direction in respect of sperm function. Under these terms we might define function as meaning the ability to fertilise an ovum. In order to fertilise an ovum, a sperm must have a number of properties, such as motility (the sperm must be motile and able to swim in a vigorous progressive fashion), good normal morphology, longevity (able to survive up to 72 hours *in vivo*), be able to become hyperactivated, able to capacitate and then undergo the acrosome reaction (which allows the sperm to penetrate the zona pellucida). Sperm function is all about a range of qualities, not just one simple property, which is why a global test is so hard to find (see Fig. 2.2). As regards the acrosome reaction, the sperm head contains the cell nucleus and several membranes, the membrane which covers the acrosome cap and the membrane covered by the acrosome cap itself. The acrosome contains enzymes which help the sperm make its way through the outer membrane of the ovum itself. The contents of the acrosome are not released unless the sperm has undergone a process called capacitation. The only way of knowing that this has occurred is when we sometimes are lucky enough to observe a normally moving sperm suddenly become hyperactivated (the sperm suddenly starts to writhe and move in an abnormal jerky fashion). Once the sperm has become hyperactivated the acrosome reaction may occur. Incidentally, after capacitation the sperm will move normally again.

Much research is currently being done on computer automated semen analysis (CASA). There is some evidence showing a correlation between curvilinear velocity (CVL) and the amplitude of head displacement (ALH) and fertilisation in IVF. The NURTURE unit in Nottingham have also used CASA (Hobson Tracker) to help them choose which sperm to use when they are doing microinsemination of sperm (more about this in Chapter 3). More needs to be done, but the expense of CASA means that currently, fewer than 10% of all IVF units have one.

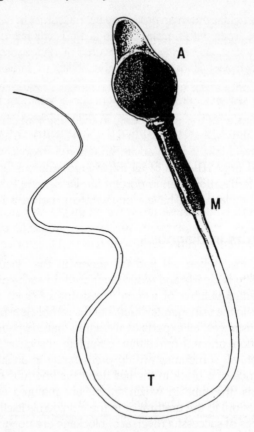

Figure 2.2 *Sperm morphology.* A mature sperm. The acrosome is contained in the uppermost portion of the sperm's head (**A**). Even now our understanding of sperm function is poor. There is a growing belief in the importance of the acrosome and a process called capacitation. The head also contains the nucleus of the sperm (the chromosomes with their genetic material), whilst the mid-piece (section just below the head, marked **M**) contains the 'engine room', which provides the energy for motility. The tail (**T**) provides the sperm with its ability to move forward and usually moves in a motion resembling that of a sine wave.

What is the meaning of fertilisation?

Once an ovum has been penetrated by a sperm, fertilisation may be deemed to have happened. In IVF we know we may confirm fertilisation by checking for the pronuclei. If normal fertilisation has occurred, we will see two nuclei (the pronuclei) appear in the egg at around 14 to 24 hours after the ovum was inseminated with sperm. Sometimes (up to 6%) we will see three pronuclei (polyspermy or triploidy arising occasionally because of ova which have not completed meiosis properly) which usually means that a second sperm has penetrated the egg. Unfortunately, such fertilisations are not useful. If fertilisation has happened normally, 80 to 90% of normally fertilised embryos will divide into two cells and then four cells.

Unfortunately, up to 50% of embryos (a dividing fertilised egg) will arrest at the 4-cell stage (i.e. showing no further development). In IVF we transfer at this stage, partly in the hope that early transfer will help the embryo avoid cleavage arrest. Only 25–40% of all normally fertilised eggs will make it to an advanced embryo stage (called blastocyst), and indeed only 10–15% of all transferred embryos produce a live baby. Thus fertilisation is an important hurdle, serving to demonstrate sperm function, but we still have a long way to go before a live birth is achieved.

Other factors in diagnosis

Of course, when we find no sperm in the ejaculate (azoospermia) infertility is clearly and easily diagnosed. In such cases there may be a substantial volume of semen (consisting of fluids from a number of glands in the urinogenital tract), but the sample is aspermic. Under these circumstances, all experts would agree that the patient is infertile. This condition arises from either complete testicular failure (sometimes congenital, sometimes arising prematurely in adulthood) or as a consequence of a block in the *vas deferens* (the tube connecting the epididymis (the tube in which sperm are matured and stored prior to ejaculation) to the urethra) or in the epididymis itself. In both cases, the chances of successful reversal of blockage are not good (often no better than a 10% success rate). Whilst a semen sample remains azoospermic there exists a definite state of infertility. Options for treatment are dealt with in Chapter 3.

Cryptorchidism, a condition where one or both the testes have failed to migrate into the scrotal sac (hence the common description of 'undescended testes') can often also result in azoospermia (even when the testes have been lowered by surgery or drugs), although in some cases function can be adequate. Where one testis is cryptorchid and the contralateral testis has descended normally, adequate sperm function may still often be demonstrated. Equally so, where one testis has been removed or in any circumstance where there remains only one functioning testis, sperm function may also still be adequate. When a testis is found to be cryptorchid during the teenage years or later still, immediate removal is recommended in order to prevent possible cancer of the testis.

When looking at male infertility of any type, we may find it additionally useful to look for normal and abnormal anatomy. In the case of normal anatomy and a positive vasogram (X-ray using radio-opaque dye) there is no surgical intervention which will be of value. In situations where abnormal anatomy is detected, for example cryptorchidism, congenital absence of *vas deferens*, or small testes there is little evidence to suggest that much may be done. In conditions such as epididymal cysts, blockage of the *vas* and varicocoele (condition where the spermatic vein, usually on the left side, is enlarged, resulting in increased blood flow to the scrotum, which is thought to raise the temperature of the scrotum from 34°C to 37°C, thereby supposedly causing spermatogenetic disruption until, in theory, the varicocoele is dealt with), surgical intervention may be considered, but even here success rates vary from nil to 25%.

Diagnosis is not complete until testicular function has been tested. The best non-surgical method is to take a sample of the male partner's blood and to measure the LH (luteinising hormone or interstitial cell stimulating hormone acting on the Leydig cells, which make testosterone), FSH (follicle stimulating hormone acts on Sertoli cells which have an intimate relationship with sperm) and testosterone (promotes sperm development) levels (Butt, 1982). Low LH or FSH levels indicate hypogonadic function, which might respond to tamoxifen, human chorionic gonadotrophin (hCG) or FSH therapy. High FSH levels are usually an indication of testicular failure. High testosterone may be an indication of testicular cancer and should be followed up by an urologist. If the endocrinology needs confirmation a testicular biopsy can be performed. So at the end of the day, if all the tests indicate absence of abnormality (endocrinological or mechanical) and surgical intervention is either not required or has been completed, provided the male partner is not azoospermic, we have to deal with what we've got.

The use of semen analysis – summary

There is the potential for misdiagnosis when using semen analysis alone in cases of oligozoospermia or asthenozoospermia alone. Nevertheless, if semen analysis alone is to be used to determine who is treatable and who is not in such circumstances, the following guidelines may be useful (Lee, 1994c).

(1) Never use a single parameter on its own. Oligozoospermia (less than 20 million per ml) alone or asthenozoospermia alone (less than 40% motility) are insufficient parameters to base a diagnosis of male infertility. Multiplying count by motility yields a useful index (the motile sperm density, MSD). As a rule of thumb, the minimum acceptable MSD in 8 million motile sperm per ml in any sample.

(2) Oligoasthenozoospermia (less than 20 million per ml and less than 40% motility, i.e. at best this would only give a motile sperm density of less than 8 million per ml) is almost untreatable.

(3) Progression, as described above is a very useful subjective para-

meter. Despite its subjectivity, progression score of less than two out of four suggest that problems lie ahead. No-one should be treated with a score of one out of four.

(4) Thus, a man with oligozoospermia of 15 million per ml and 80% motility (MSD of 12 million per ml) should be treatable, but a man with the same count, but 50% motility should be dissuaded if possible (7.5 million per ml). Similarly, an asthenozoospermic man with count of 30 million per ml and 20% motility would be dissuaded from having treatment (MSD of only 6 million per ml), whilst a man with the same motility, but with a count of 80 million per ml would happily be offered treatment (MSD 16 million per ml).

Ideally, these guidelines are best used in conjunction with tests of sperm function such as swim up testing or mucus testing (see Erian & Lee, 1990; Jennings & Lee, 1995). Thus even if the semen analysis guidelines above are passed:

- If a swim up preparation test produces less than 500 000 per ml and/ or less than 80% motility, the patient should not be offered invasive, expensive treatment
- If PCT is poor or negative, as above
- If the sperm–mucus test is poor or negative, as above
- If mucus penetration of 11 mm or less is obtained, as above

Other tests of sperm function

The use of swim up testing (using IVF methodology to carry out test preparations) provides a very useful second line of screening, which in addition to sperm-mucus testing (Kremer-type testing is best as quantitative results may be obtained) provides sufficient data for accurate diagnosis of sperm function or dysfunction. The post-coital test (PCT), provided it is well timed, is also useful. The time of ovulation is best determined by serial ultrasound scanning. The PCT is performed six to ten hours post coitus. Mucus from both the internal os and the low cervix should be examined. The test is positive if ten motile sperm per high power field are observed ($\times$ 40 objective). It is important to determine how well the sperm survive in the mucus.

This should be followed by a sperm-mucus contact test (SMCT). A donor sperm (which is of proven fertility, i.e. sperm function) cross check should also help to reveal clues to sperm dysfunction (i.e. if the mucus is poor the donor sperm will show this up). One way of carrying out the SMCT is to apply a small sample of mucus to a slide. This can then be covered with a cover slip. A small sample of semen may be applied at the edge of the cover slip. Once again, the test is positive when ten sperm per high power field can be seen to have penetrated the mucus and to be making tracks across it. Mucus volume, ferning, consistency and Spinnbarkeit should also be noted. Finally, the mucus should be checked for leukocytes and the pH determined. Low pH immobilises sperm, whilst optimal mid-cycle mucus has a pH ranging from 7.0 to 8.5. Mucus sperm function tests are only unreliable when the mucus is of poor quality (i.e. sperm function may be adequate), so great care must be taken to obtain good quality mucus. Ideally, for standardisation and to control against poor mucus quality, donor mucus and semen should be obtainable in large amounts so that cross checks may also be carried out.

Antisperm antibodies in men

No testing is complete until antisperm antibody presence in the semen has been excluded. Presence of antibodies do not necessarily imply infertility, but their presence is likely to complicate matters. In some cases, the ejaculate is thick and very viscous. About 50% of all cases involving viscous semen will result in antisperm antibodies being detected and is usually due to the presence of very severe agglutination. However on the other side of the coin only about 50% of all antibody cases demonstrate viscous semen. Specific diagnosis is difficult as there are many types of antibody such as IgG, IgA, IgM antibodies to head, midpiece and tail (see also Lee, 1990), which may bind to many different types of antigens on the sperm. It is possible that some types of antibody may bind to the sperm heads, thereby interfering with fertilisation, but fortunately this does not occur very often (about 10–15% of times). Often the antibodies cause severe agglutination when IgG and IgA are both present in large amounts (more than 50% immunobead binding to both IgG and IgA), but not cytotoxicity unless we introduce non-heat inactivated serum to the medium, or bind to the sperm tails, thereby interfering with motility (producing poor progression). When IgG and IgA are both present together, the antibodies may bind to both head and tail as well as cross reacting to produce severe agglutination. An antibody of the IgG type, in the absence of IgA, tends to bind to tail only.

Cases involving IgA alone are rare in males. Routine tests for antibodies involve the use of antibody-sensitive round latex particles. These will stick tightly to the sperm if they have antibodies on them. The two commercially available tests are SpermMar (produced by Fertipro, Ghent, Belgium) and immunobeads (made by BioRad, Hemel Hempstead, UK).

When antibodies are present, except in cases where antibody binding to the head is present, their main effect is to cause agglutination or poor progression. In cases of agglutination, huge amounts of sperm are removed from the reproductive arena, leaving few 'untagged' sperm to achieve their objective. So, if we are able to reduce the agglutination, more sperm would therefore become available (more about this in Chapter 3).

When agglutination is the complicating factor in antibody presence, IVF treatment success is relatively common regarding pregnancy. However, about 90% of these pregnancies result in miscarriage (Lee, unpublished data). Generally, these miscarriages are commonly diagnosed as blighted ovum at 7–11 weeks of pregnancy. Some will also manifest as ectopic pregnancies. Reasons for this are unclear.

Part of the solution may lie in the fact that polyspermy (eggs fertilised by more than one sperm) is common when agglutinating sperm antibodies are present (Lee, unpublished observation). It is possible that in IVF treatment for such cases, we are not being careful enough with our semen preparation. Although we are culling out the severest clumps of agglutinated sperm, we may still be allowing too many doublets (two sperm stuck together by an antibody) into our inseminating preparations. These may be able to fertilise ova, thereby producing triploid embryos, which may be more likely to produce ectopics and blighted ova pregnancies (more research needs to be done to confirm this hypothesis, which the author presented to the Society for the Study of Fertility in York during the summer meeting of 1987). There is support for this idea, as Richard Bronson in the USA (Bronson *et al.*, 1990) has shown that hamster egg penetration tests become extremely enhanced in some antibody cases.

When IgG is present alone, its main effect is to make sperm preparation difficult. Because the sperm are sluggish, they will not swim up well. I therefore always expect previously undiagnosed antibody presence if I am told of a surprising case of failure to fertilise in IVF, where a normal semen analysis has been reported. Even though the semen analysis is normal, because the sperm are sluggish a poor preparation will be obtained, which (poor semen preparation) in my experience, accounts for over 90% of all failure to fertilise cases in IVF (which is why a swim-up preparation test is also a good test of sperm function). A great deal more study is needed in this area.

Other problems

I would like to say a little more here about viscous samples. Obviously, when antibodies are present, the way of dealing with the semen samples is to get the men to ejaculate into pots containing medium (about 10 ml), which helps to dilute the antibodies, thereby helping to reduce viscosity. It may also help to triturate (using a rubber teated pipette to draw in and then expel the semen repeatedly) the semen vigorously for about three minutes. If this fails, leave the sample pot on a heated rack (37°C) for 30 minutes and/or add medium and then triturate again. Viscous semen produces reduced fertility by mathematically reducing the number of active sperm available for fertilisation, because the sperm are unable to escape from the thick seminal plasma. Thus, by reducing viscosity we are helping to overcome a relatively simple problem, hence cervical or intrauterine insemination should prove most effective for this problem.

Round cell presence is a contentious issue in seminology. Historically, round cells are almost always interpreted as being evidence of infection. However, microbiological culture rarely confirms the presence of pathogens. There are possibly two reasons for this. First, semen being highly immunosuppressive, it may be that the pathogens are not being appropriately transported to the growth media (i.e. if in doubt mix suspect semen with IUI/IVF medium in a ratio $1:1$ (v/v) and then transport the prospective pathogen to the growth plates/tubes), or secondly, the round cells are not pus cells. Generally, when the count is oligozoospermic, round cell count of more than four million per ml is an indication of germ cell presence and testicular failure. When the count is normal and the sample reveals moderate asthenozoospermia (severe asthenozoospermia usually indicates spermatogenic or spermiogenic disruption) and round cell count is more than 4 million per ml, one should suspect infection, unless the patient reports high alcohol or smoking intake. In my experience infected semen samples occur less than 2% of the time in a routine infertility investigative laboratory, so routine use of Septrin, Flagyl or erythromycin is unwarranted when round cells are observed in semen samples. Take care with microbiological technique and take a detailed history from the patient before taking action.

On completing diagnosis, we are then in a position to apply treatment, if necessary. Sometimes there is no obvious element of sperm dysfunction, in which case there is no reason to offer treatment unless there is a clear female factor. When all the above have been tested for and excluded, even though we may not understand the underlying pathology, we usually have to work with what we've got.

How do specialists, male or female, deal with men with confirmed diagnosis of male infertility?

Before concluding this chapter, I must make a small mention about male infertility and how it affects not only patients but also the doctors and specialists dealing with them. There are those who are able to deal with a patient in a professional and sympathetic manner, and then there are those who handle the situation badly.

Some specialists deny that a problem exists. Even when sperm function is absent, the man will be told that either the count or motility (or both) is a little low, but that it is okay. It is possible that this type of scenario is a consequence of ignorance and lack of training in this area (formal training in infertility remains rare, even today), but it is also possible that the denial is rooted with an inability or reluctance to deal with such issues. It is interesting to note that male and female GPs and/or gynaecologists are both equally guilty of the above. There is obviously some hidden agenda relating to this phenomenon. One might speculate that the stigma of male infertility is so strong that both men and women, who are likely to have grown up with their appropriate role models with different ideologies (male or female), are equally appalled by the lot of men with a destiny of diminished prospects of parenthood. Whatever the reasons, causes for the denial remain unclear.

Diagnosing psychogenic impotence

Before finishing this chapter, we should consider impotence, which may be common in cases of male infertility. It is useful for both the male and the female partner to attend the first consultation, but readers might be surprised at how often the male partner is absent during a first appointment in the gynaecology infertility clinic. Here we are dealing with psychogenic impotence, which usually occurs suddenly. Organic impotence tends to be a progressive disorder except in cases of spinal injury and will not be dealt in this book, as it is a particularly specialised area, which is best left to urological surgeons with a special interest.

The partner's response is important. An understanding sympathetic reaction in the female partner will help to make the impotence a transient affair, whilst a demanding insecure insistent partner is likely to exacerbate the problem. Specific sexual history interview is vital in helping to point out possible pathways of intervention. Episodes of impotence are often associated with 'having to perform' (performance anxiety), so some cases involve normal erections in all activities save penetration. Knowing whether erectile dysfunction is absolute or not is useful. Counselling is a very effective way of dealing with psychogenic impotence.

Conclusion

I hope that the contents of this chapter will be useful in providing a basis for anyone working within the field of male infertility. Most importantly, I hope I have been able to impress upon all readers that we urgently need to agree on standards for assessing sperm function, for it is not until we have a global test of sperm function that we will all be talking the same language. Once we are able to assess sperm with standard and meaningful tests, I believe that our understanding and ability to treat male infertility will undergo a quantum leap.

Diagnosis of male infertility remains somewhat in the dark ages. Not only because of a continuing lack of knowledge or understanding. There is now sufficient expertise available to carry out frontline research on sperm function, but the problem seems to lie in the willingness of people to learn what is known and to apply the knowledge to the benefit of their patients. As pointed out above, there remain too many doctors and specialists who would rather not deal with this common condition. It is possible that we will actually have to deal with the psychological aspect of male infertility as it is perceived in society before we will be able to fully grasp the nettle in overcoming the inertia that clearly persists in making male infertility one of society's great taboo subjects.

Chapter 3
Treatment Options for Male Infertility

Introduction

Treatments for infertility in general have not to date been subjected to sufficient large controlled studies, in order to demonstrate efficacy. It is generally accepted that no treatment option currently provides more than about 10% live birth rates per treatment cycle, in spite of what is claimed by individual units (refer to Human Fertilisation and Embryology Authority (HFEA) annual reports of 1992, 1993 and 1994). All treatments are therefore unproven quantities. Nevertheless, the public interest and media interest ensure a never ending stream of patients willing to act as guinea-pigs for whatever treatment option might be the flavour of the month. Furthermore, it has become very clear to me that for many couples, there is more to the treatment than meets the eye (see later chapters). Thus, for those who feel they must obtain medical intervention, the field of assisted reproduction/conception beckons.

This chapter seeks to outline in modest terms (it is not meant to be comprehensive by any stretch of the imagination), the main treatment options that couples might expect to face in their quest to become parents. All are used for male infertility (as well as for many other indications), but are not exclusively so. I start the chapter by looking at the treatment of more esoteric problems before moving on to the mainstream treatment options for the more common male infertilities. I have left out surgical treatments from this chapter, which are generally provided by urological surgeons (for more information see Anne Jequier's excellent book (1986) titled *Infertility in the Male*. As I have pointed out in Chapter 2, results are variable and often unsuccessful. Where success is achieved, there is unlikely to be a need for further treatment, except in cases of vasectomy reversal, when almost universally the men will have antibodies to sperm present in their semen.

For further details on treatment options see the following reviews: Davies *et al.* (1988), Hull (1991), Lee (1988a,b; 1991a; 1995c).

Treating impotence

Impotence was discussed briefly at the end of Chapter 2, so it seems only fair to deal with it first here. Impotence may arise as a consequence of infertility or indeed may be a cause of it. More is said about its importance as a corollary to male infertility in later chapters. Certainly, impotence is a topic which arouses fear and anxiety in men. Howsoever it arises, so long as it is not caused by an organic problem (for instance a mechanical problem such as neuropathy or circulatory/vascular disorders), it is important to determine a few facts. In these cases knowledge of the patient's previous libido, ejaculatory pattern and experience of orgasm is important so that an assessment may be made (in comparison with current experience) of the components making up the current disorder. Information on when sexual problems began and whether they were gradual or sudden is also useful, as is current information regarding coital frequency, if any, erection during masturbation, or drug use (an example of dealing with impotence is demonstrated in Case History 3.1 below).

Case history 3.1

Mr J attended the clinic for treatment with respect to his impotence. Until his diagnosis of male infertility, he had had no problems at all, but since then, he had had several episodes of impotence. Erection was normal and ejaculation was possible and normal when he masturbated, but when he tried to have sex with his partner, erectile dysfunction was becoming increasingly common. The couple's sex life, which had been active (five to six times a month) was becoming less frequent. Mr J had not taken any drugs, except for paracetamol or aspirin, during the past three years prior to the problem of impotence.

Mr J contracted to have four sessions of counselling. Mrs J never attended any of the sessions. During the first session, we explored the issue of guilt and blame. Mr J did not immediately embrace these ideas, but agreed they might be relevant. He was much more interested in the idea of performance-related anxiety and the increasing feeling of futility of 'meaningless sex', as he put it. The fact that he now began to feel that 'normal sex' was not going to work, the futility of sex was affecting his performance. It became clear that sex was an important symbol for Mr J and that meaningless sex was a turn off for him.

In the second session, we discussed how he viewed his wife and the state of their relationship at 'this moment in time'. He reported that his wife was still sexually desirable and that they had a good strong relationship. On reflection, he had spent some time reflecting on the contents of the first session and now felt that he did feel very guilty about his inability to father a child. He also confided that he had recently started to have panic attacks about the idea that his wife might decide to ditch him for someone else, who might be able to give her a baby.

Case history 3.1 *continued*

In the third session, we began to look at strategies. He had been working through the previous sessions with his wife and he felt that she would be happy to try and be more sexy during their lovemaking. Because he had no problems with erection during masturbation, we looked at the possibility of just spending a few weeks where penetrative sex was banned and Mr and Mrs J would just enjoy mutual masturbation. Mr J was told that he should progress on to full sex whenever he felt ready. We looked at the idea of using videos or magazines to enhance his excitement prior to joining his wife in their bedroom, but he felt this would not be helpful. Finally, we agreed that he would just try to enjoy sex again and to try not to think about the failure to conceive; indeed to try to divorce the idea of sex and reproduction (ironic, since it would be so much better if more couples would think seriously about reproduction through sex and not through assisted reproduction technology), so that his performance related anxiety might be dispelled. (It is amazing how the idea of sex and reproduction is so deeply rooted in the psyche. Is this the fault of religion – 'Go forth and multiply'?)

Mr J rang to cancel his fourth appointment and as far as I am aware has had no subsequent problems.

In treatment terms, during counselling it is important to overcome conflict. For psychogenic impotence, empirical treatments with testosterone, yohimbine or isoxsuprine may prove of value. Sex therapy is also often appropriate therapy (in particular consider sensate focus).

Sensate focus

This is a set of exercises popularised by Masters and Johnson, involving a predetermined set of exercises which clients agree to undergo according to a prescribed pattern. It is particularly useful in cases of impotence, as well as for other types of sexual dysfunction.

In brief, sensate focus involves a ban on full penetrative sex at the start. The client is encouraged to focus on exploring the sensations of feeling and touching. To begin with, certain parts of the body will be placed 'off-limits', but as the exercises progress, the couple are allowed to move on to other exercises, until finally full sex is allowed to take place. There is a further consideration of this in Chapter 5.

The following matters are also relevant to the treatment of impotence. For mechanical problems, papaverine injections or penile prostheses are in routine use. The first is a pharmacological method involving injection into the penis. A major complication is occasional priapism (blood in the erect penis stays trapped therein resulting in prolonged erection, which may be 'cured' by aspiration of the blood). The second method involves surgical implantation of a prosthesis.

Treating patients with spinal injuries

This is an area where infertility due to impotence often has a clear mechanical (organic) root. Semen samples are usually obtained by electroejaculation (a procedure which may be uncomfortable for some). Success in these circumstances is variable. The sample will then be used for cervical insemination (unprepared semen).

My own experience consists of work carried out over 24 months in collaboration with two urologists Mr Julian Shaw and Mr Anthony Timoney (Timoney, Lee & Shaw, 1990) at the spinal injuries unit in Stanmore, Middlesex. Here we had seven patients with severe spinal injuries. Most had experienced electroejaculation and elected to discontinue with treatment. Spermatoceles (implants which are attached to the *vas deferens*) were used to act as sperm reservoirs. These devices were then aspirated by means of a needle and syringe. Indeed, we were able routinely to aspirate motile sperm from these spermatoceles. The patients were taught to aspirate the spermatoceles and to perform self insemination (without preparation) in their own homes. During a 12 month trial period, no pregnancies resulted. Treatment was complicated by occasional contamination of aspirates by blood. For the next 12 months a mixture of home treatment was mixed with visits to the clinic for study on the status of the spermatoceles.

During the first 12 months of the study, half of the patients experienced increasing problems with the spermatoceles. Several became completely blocked and had to be replaced, the others became contaminated with blood more often. Subsequent study during the final 12 months showed that motility of the samples improved significantly if the spermatoceles were flushed with medium containing glucose. The glucose was clearly an important key component. Medium without glucose did not produce improvement in motility, yet when present, every semen sample revealed improved motility (from 0 or 1% motility to 10% motility and from 5% motility to 30%). During the second 12 months of the study, no pregnancies were achieved. Subsequent study showed that the reservoirs were toxic to sperm (P. Matson, personal communication), as a result of their design. However, we concluded from our experience that the spermatoceles were worth persisting with, but more active intervention was needed; for example careful timing of insemination allied to sperm preparation and intrauterine insemination (IUI). This line of management may now also be enhanced by the addition of microepididymal sperm aspiration–intracytoplasmic sperm injection (MESA–ICSI) or Biopsy–ICSI (see later section on intracytoplasmic sperm injection (ICSI) in this chapter).

Options for idiopathic male infertility

Prior to the advent of ICSI, there were few treatments worth considering in cases of male infertility. Every man given a diagnosis of infertility (rightly or mistakenly) will report the option of DI being offered almost immediately (with varying degrees of sympathy and sensitivity). Other than this, little more was usually on offer. Over the years cervical insemination of the unprepared sample was offered (with success rates of between 3–10% per treatment cycle). Intrauterine insemination (IUI), gamete intrafallopian transfer (GIFT) and *in vitro* fertilisation (IVF) have also been offered, but again with variable results. My own beliefs prior to ICSI, were that if we have a case of male infertility *per se*, why inflict more misery on the female partner, and why raise hopes in couples with as much chance of success when left to their own devices as they would have with the treatment (approximately 15% of couples with untreated male infertility will still succeed in having a child over a two year study period, see Hull, 1991). Furthermore, GIFT and IVF require surgery with all its known risks and complications.

Donor insemination (DI)

To provide a DI service, a clinic must now be licensed by the HFEA. Additionally, it must recruit donors in order to have semen available for use. Donors are relatively hard to recruit and have short-lived careers, since they are allowed a maximum of ten pregnancies, after which their semen may no longer be used. Donor recruitment is therefore somewhat haphazard. Even though the HFEA provides strict guidelines, there remains a degree of latitude so that the quality of donors from clinic to clinic is subject to considerable variation. Screening for sexually transmitted disease, common bacterial, fungal and virus infections should all be done on a routine basis. Genetic screening is also a prerequisite. Age, physical characteristics, character, etc. may all be taken into consideration, but cut-off points will almost certainly differ from clinic to clinic, perhaps according to whether their bank is well filled or not.

Because most DI clinics rely on traditional semen analysis, (remember, even when the semen analysis is good, up to 10% of such samples may still fail to fertilise ova in IVF treatment) the quality of the donor samples is subject to large variation. In my own experience, encompassing over 300 cycles of donor semen use in GIFT, IVF or IUI, I have found that 50% of semen samples from large donor banks will not have provided a pregnancy, even after they have been used at least five times. In other words, only one half of donor samples in use at any one time are likely to be of proven value. Furthermore, when donors over 38 years of age are used, pregnancy rates will be of the order of 1–2% (Lee, unpublished data). Thus, there is an argument for donors to be tested for sperm function rather than by semen analysis only. Clinics need to improve their screening and selection criteria in the future in order to safeguard patients and their prospective success rates.

The latest HFEA report reveals a live birth rate for all UK DI clinics of just 5%, which is somewhat disappointing. There has been little or no public debate about such poor results. Current practice, once a donor has been recruited, is to bank samples by freezing the semen. An average ejaculate of 3 ml would be mixed with 3 ml of a special fluid containing cryoprotectant. The resulting 6 ml of fluid would be divided into 12 plastic straws, each containing 0.5 ml, which would be placed into liquid nitrogen and stored there until use. The straws are not released for use until 6 months quarantine has passed (during which time, the donor will have been screened for various diseases including HIV at three-monthly intervals). Donor insemination treatment then consists of cervical insemination of unprepared frozen–thawed semen samples. The DI is done either mid cycle, timed according to LH surge or timed by ultrasound scanning, depending on the practice of the clinic. There are therefore, a number of factors which might explain poor results. Results will depend on age of patients, quality of patients, timing of insemination, quality of resources put into the treatment. Thus older patients will fare poorly, as will patients who have additional factors (one tube only, endometriosis, irregular cycles, etc.) and whose timing of insemination is inaccurate. There are also strong arguments for the use of ovarian stimulation and more importantly the use of intrauterine insemination following preparation of the frozen–thawed semen sample.

Freezing–thawing damages sperm

I have previously published the fact (Jennings & Lee, 1995) that freezing and thawing semen causes significant reduction in sperm function, as revealed by mucus penetration testing. My recommendation that frozen–thawed samples should only be used after semen preparation is based on this fact. What might corroborate my statement? Prior to HIV and AIDS, many clinics used fresh donor semen on a routine basis. Many of these clinics used to report 10% live birth rates on a routine basis. Indeed, these results were achieved with very poor resources, as the timing of insemination was far less accurate in those days. These same clinics have reported a substantial reduction in success rates following the mandatory introduction of the use of frozen–thawed quarantined semen samples only. This suggests that the introduction of quarantined semen samples has contributed significantly to current poor live birth rates.

How can we substantiate the use of semen preparation? My own experience with IVF and GIFT has shown me that after couples who have tried IVF with the husband's semen, in spite of a diagnosis of severe male infertility, have produced poor fertilisation rates and failed to produce a baby, they will almost certainly elect to undertake further treatment with either donor semen IVF or GIFT. If the female partner has no diagnosable infertility, this action is somewhat questionable, but I shall not dwell on it here. Suffice it to say that it is a common enough occurrence in every IVF clinic. The important thing to consider here is that these couples who with the husband's semen have previously been producing live birth rates of less than 3% per treatment cycle, will suddenly produce live birth rates of 20 and 35% with IVF and GIFT respectively by choosing the donor option. The vast majority (more than 95%) of all IVF and GIFT done with donor semen in my experience have used frozen–thawed semen (Lee, unpublished data). Yet we get such good results; why? To carry out IVF or GIFT we must use prepared semen. I suggest therefore, the action of preparation does not repair the damage, rather that by preparation we are able to separate the sperm which are still active and viable from the damaged ones. Because in IVF and GIFT we are dealing with hundreds of thousands rather than millions as in the case of DI normally, preparation overcomes the problems of damage by freezing–thawing. If we are to use prepared sperm for DI, because we are culling out such large numbers of poor sperm, it is logical to propose that the sperm be placed directly into the uterus by IUI. I believe that the use of donor intrauterine insemination (DIUI) with prepared semen would, at the very least, double current live birth rates! One colleague (W.A.R. Davies, of Northampton General Hospital, personal communication) who undertook the use of DIUI in a study comparing it with traditional DI, found that his DIUI live birth rate was about two to three times that of his DI success rate.

Empirical superovulation (ES)

For patients unwilling to consider DI and who have some motile sperm (minimum of one million motile sperm) other options may be considered. More recently, the author set up a trial to see if empirical drug therapy (as usual the female partner has to endure this as with all treatments in spite of the infertility being related to the male) might be useful in these circumstances (Mascarenhas *et al.*, 1994). The simple rationale is that if there are more eggs there might be a better chance of success. With empirical superovulation (ES), the female partner is given daily injections of gonadotrophins (drugs that promote multiple follicle development in the ovaries). The response of the ovaries is monitored regularly by ultrasound. When two to three mature follicles are seen, a final injection of human chorionic gonadotrophin (hCG) is given to produce ovulation. After this the couple are advised to have sex in the next 24 to 48 hours. If there are more than four mature follicles, hCG is withheld and the cycle is abandoned because the chances of a risky multiple pregnancy become too high (although multiple pregnancy in cases of male infertility are very rare).

Regrettably, the study showed the use of fertility drugs on the female, in cases of male infertility, was not of value. Nevertheless, in the district general hospital (DGH), ES is often the limit of treatment options available for all categories of infertility, so in spite of the results reported by Mascarenhas *et al.* (1994), some couples are still likely to be offered ES for their male infertility in the years to come. At best, perhaps ES may have some value in the way of offering couples encouragement, since they may at least feel that something is being done for them (albeit of no value).

Use of fertility drugs on men is discussed later in this chapter.

Intrauterine insemination (IUI)

These days, the first port of call, if intervention is requested, might be IUI in conjunction with fertility drugs (called superovulation). The treatment is called IUI with empirical superovulation (empirical because the method is still unproven). In fact the author's own data shows that in a controlled prospective study involving 64 couples, IUI and ES was no better than ES and timed intercourse (Lee & Mascarenhas, 1993). Nevertheless, it is still routinely on offer to couples, including those with joint presence of both male and female factors, who should be suitable for IUI and ES so long as tubal patency is demonstrable. Such couples who have failed with ES may benefit from 3–6 cycles of IUI with ES.

This treatment is also suitable for idiopathics (unexplained) who are not having sex or who are not achieving penetration during sex. Patients will still be given ES, but instead of just having sex, after hCG is given, the couple will attend the clinic 36 hours after hCG, in order to have the IUI. The male partner produces a semen sample, which undergoes preparation. The best sperm are then placed in the female partner's uterus by means of a transcervical catheter, thereby by-passing the cervix. The IUI is a simple procedure that is usually painless, quick and does not require general or local anaesthesia or surgery. Again, as per ES alone, IUI is of little real benefit in cases of male infertility on its own, unless a cervical factor or antisperm antibodies are present. In cases involving antibodies to sperm in the male, IUI is an entirely appropriate treatment, but the semen sample must be produced into a pot containing 10 ml of medium. This medium helps by dispersing the antibody, thereby reducing the number of 'tagged' sperm and in cases of IgG + IgA will also reduce the amount of clumping. Thereafter, the semen is still prepared using the swim-up method (see Fig. 3.1).

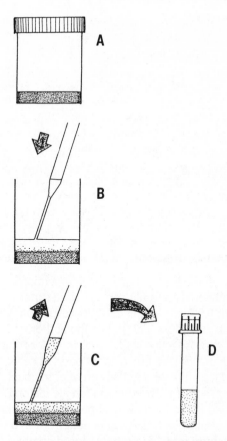

Figure 3.1 *Direct migration semen preparation.* Depiction of a simple method of semen preparation. The method relies on the strongly motile sperms swimming into the upper layer of medium. The rationale behind this method of preparation is that the immotile and poorly progressive sperms will be 'culled' out of the preparation, leaving behind a preparation containing an enhanced percentage of viable ones.

A: the semen sample is in the pot; **B**: the fresh medium is gently placed over the sample; **C**: after 15–45 minutes of incubation at 37°C, the upper layer of medium is drawn off; **D**: the preparation is placed in a test tube and is now ready for insemination.

Patients failing ES and IUI

After six cycles of IUI with ES, about 40–70% (70% if male infertility) of couples will still have failed. Many will find themselves offered GIFT or IVF. More commonly, these days IVF. In my opinion, IVF is for tubals only. If there is tubal patency, ES alone should be sufficient, so long as male factors are absent. Thus GIFT should only be considered after ES failure, at the earliest, since most couples may also benefit from IUI with ES (up to six cycles). In some circumstances, where poor sperm or egg quality is suspected, a diagnostic IVF cycle may be useful before trying GIFT.

With GIFT, the female partner is superovulated as per ES (but with higher doses as more eggs are required since multiple pregnancies are limited by restricting transfer to a maximum of three ova), but after hCG, instead of sex or insemination, egg recovery takes place 36 hours after hCG; three eggs (chosen for maturity and for absence of damage) are then placed with prepared sperm directly into the fallopian tube, immediately egg recovery is completed. After three cycles, 20–60% (20% with male infertility) of couples will have conceived a baby.

Direct oocyte transfer (DOT) is a procedure just like GIFT. It differs only in the site where the eggs and prepared sperm are placed immediately after egg recovery. The site of transfer in this case is the uterus. This technique is therefore suited to all couples who have tried and failed IUI with ES, as well as those with blocked tubes. An argument may be made that up to three cycles of DOT should be tried before IVF referral. The technique is currently used routinely in only one clinic in the UK, as far as I am aware. It is offered to patients in Colchester by my good friend and colleague Ian Treharne, and myself. To date, I have myself carried out over 100 DOTs, resulting in more than 15 babies delivered (all singleton pregnancies, except for one pair of twins; approximately a 10% procedure), though, at present it must still be considered to be experimental.

In vitro fertilisation (IVF)

IVF is the first port of call for patients with tubal disease, if they are unsuitable for tubal surgery or choose not to consider it. It may also be suitable for some of the other categories of female infertility, after prolonged treatment with less stressful and invasive options such as IUI with ES or GIFT. It is contraindicated in cases of severe male factors unless done in conjunction with sperm and egg manipulation (see below). As with GIFT, IVF requires superovulation, egg recovery and semen preparation. However, the eggs and sperm are kept in a dish in the laboratory for 48 hours, instead of being transferred immediately after egg recovery. Therefore, with IVF, we may tell whether there has been fertilisation or not (the sperm being able to penetrate the egg – failure of penetration means that nothing will be transferred and the IVF has failed). If fertilisation has occurred, up to three embryos will be placed in the uterus transcervically, using a special catheter (similar to IUI). After 3 cycles 20–60% (20% for male infertility) of couples will have delivered a baby.

Further treatment options

In severe cases of male infertility, it is likely apart from DI that none of the aforementioned methods will be suitable. However, since 1991, the following new possibilities have been developed; all these methods must be done in conjunction with IVF:

Microepididymal sperm aspiration (MESA) allows sperm to be obtained from azoospermic men, with vasal absence or blockage. This procedure requires surgery. A fine needle may be inserted into the epididymis allowing some motile sperm to be extracted. This sperm is then prepared and used for IVF.

Intracytoplasmic sperm injection (ICSI) is carried out when the sperm count or motility is very poor. Sperm may be picked up using a very fine needle and injected into the egg direct. The injected egg is then subjected to IVF.

Biopsy–ICSI is the same as above, except that the sperm used are derived from testicular biopsy. Here a fine needle is inserted into the testes directly in order to extract sperm for injection.

Electroejaculation is used for men with impotence or who are spinally injured. Usually the semen obtained in this way will be prepared and used for IUI, GIFT or IVF.

However, if there is some evidence of residual sperm function (i.e. swim up is just adequate or a few sperm are able to penetrate mucus), IUI, IVF or GIFT may be offered depending on the severity of dysfunction. The key to treatment lies in the quality of the preparation (the hunt for and isolation of the elite sperm). In my opinion, if there is no obvious female factor, IVF and GIFT are still questionable treatment options for male factor infertility.

Empirical options for men

Other empirical treatments may be of value, but these have not been proven in controlled studies. Tamoxifen, mesterolone, gonadotrophin injections, hCG and vitamin supplements may all be given to the male patient and are popular supplementary therapies, especially with urologists. The tamoxifen is useful in cases where the blood levels of the sex hormones are normal. In these cases, tamoxifen (dose of 20 mg twice daily for 30– 60 days) may raise the count significantly. Sperm quality is rarely improved, but you certainly get more of the same (useful perhaps if considering semen preparation and IUI). Mesterolone is usually only of value if the testosterone levels are below 15 nM. In these cases, motility is usually poor (and is often associated with greater than 4 million per ml germ cell presence in the semen). Twenty five milligrams of mesterolone on a daily basis for 60 days should then boost testosterone levels and the percentage motility. The use of gonadotrophins or hCG may be of benefit. Here the rationale is that they probably will not have any effect, but their use will not hurt. Courses of treatment are usually given for three months prior to assisted conception. Finally, more recently, methods have relied on medium supplements. Pentoxyfylline and taurine have been used to 'supercharge' sperm (possibly converting some of the poorer sperm into crack troops) during semen preparation, whilst some specialists also add vitamin E to the preparation media.

ICSI: A new twist to the tale

Here we shall look at the development of ICSI, how it is done and how it may change practice in the future. Intracytoplasmic sperm injection, MESA–ICSI and Biopsy–ICSI seem set to revolutionise infertility treatment as a whole, whereby it threatens to dominate the field of infertility in the 1990s. Not just for male infertility, but for all treatment aspects. Quite simply, ICSI allows embryologists to pick up individual sperm and to inject them directly into the egg. Obviously, initially, it was thought that this was an option only for men with very severe male infertility. However, the experience of Professor Van Steirteghem, whose team in Belgium has shown results of up to 30% live birth rates per embryo transfer are possible with men who have poor semen quality. The possibility that even better results will be achieved with other categories of infertility need urgent investigation. It is possible that male infertility diagnosis may be rendered obsolete by the method, couples electing to receive treatment direct, thereby foregoing the specific diagnosis, in favour of instant treatment. Case History 3.2 concerns a couple who had tried ICSI.

Case history 3.2

Mr and Mrs O had tried everything. They had sought treatment throughout the home counties, experiencing IUI, DI, IVF with and without donor semen, and ICSI. After nine years of involuntary infertility and continuing childlessness, they had seemingly reached the end of the trail. They came for counselling, it seemed to me as a last resort, since they were now at a loss as to where they went from here.

(It is not uncommon for me to see couples such as Mr and Mrs O. In 1994 alone I counselled six couples who had been through the same experience. In two of the cases, I was seeing couples who I had first seen at least five years ago, when they had felt then, that they were at the end of the line. Reproduction technology, therefore has a tremendous hold on

---

Case history 3.2 *continued*

people, because it moves on inexorably. As Strathern (1992) put it so well, the technology keeps on promising the future fulfilment of all man's desires, because technology promises hope in the future and because 'there are seemingly no barriers to what is open to artificial intervention'. Thus on the one hand the ethical and moral debate seems destined never to catch up, whilst equally so on the other hand, because we all naturally project into the future, it is my experience that this makes it almost impossible for some men and women to 'let go' of treatment. Thus, even when a couple have let go, there may eventually be a new treatment on offer promising new hope that brings couples back to the fold.)

Mr and Mrs O told me their story. It was a sad story – at times it had its highs, but inevitably the highs led to lows. The couple had certainly ridden a roller coaster and were now left drained both physically and mentally. Furthermore, they were obviously confused about what the future held in store for them.

The counselling sessions that followed looked at the issue of the reality of facing childlessness. We also looked at how the couple viewed their desires for the future and what it meant to them, as a whole. A number of coping strategies were discussed and we also explored ways in which they might marshal their resources to carry on.

As far as I am aware, at the six month review, the couple are still childless. They seem to be coping and are obviously still trying for a child naturally and for the present seem happy with their choice to let sleeping dogs lie for the time being rather than to chase further options.

As mentioned earlier in the book, there is still no global method of sperm function testing. In recent years, several companies and a number of medical scientists, John Aitken, David Katz, James Overstreet, Don Wolf, Harry Moore and David Mortimer, to name just a few, have tried to develop computer assisted methods. Computer methods rely on image analysis, which is costly to develop. Image analysis requires expensive hardware, a video camera, computer, software and intensive development time. As a consequence, automated analysers capable of reproducible standardised results are very expensive (about £20 000 per machine). Because the cost of the hardware and of the tests is considerable there is therefore a real possibility that computer-automated semen assessment will become just a research tool rather than the special diagnostic tool that was expected. The arguments will be made therefore that it is cheaper to just go ahead with treatment (the cost of hardware for ICSI is over £40 000).

How is ICSI done and what are the principles behind the idea?

With ICSI, the preparation for treatment is the same as for GIFT or IVF.

The difference is that, when the egg collection is done, instead of conventional IVF (where about 50 000–100 000 sperm are used to inseminate an ovum in the culture dish), a single sperm may be chosen, taking up into a very fine glass needle (about 0.0007 cm in diameter) and then injected (see Fig. 3.2) directly into the ovum (mature egg). The injected ovum is then placed into a culture dish as per standard IVF. The next day the ovum would be checked for signs of fertilisation and then transferred 24 hours later if this had occurred. The key part of ICSI therefore is the injection procedure, the rest being the same as for normal IVF. Moving sperm is not a prerequisite for ICSI, but it is for conventional IVF.

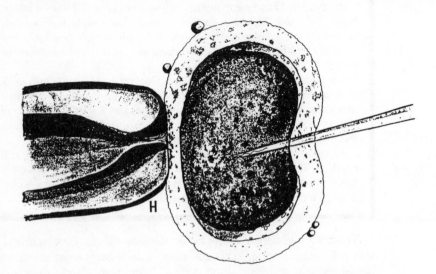

Figure 3.2 *ICSI.* A sperm is drawn into the barrel of a very fine glass needle (~7 μ in diameter). The sperm is then injected into the cytoplasm of an egg. The needle can be seen in the very centre of the egg in the illustration and a sperm may be seen to be just moving out of the barrel. The object marked (**H**) opposite the needle and immediately next to the egg, is the holding pipettet, which helps to stabilise the egg during the microinjection procedure. This novel technique may be a revolutionary way of overcoming male infertility.

As with ICSI alone, both MESA and Biopsy forms of ICSI involve surgery in order to extract sperm from the epididymis or the testes themselves. MESA (microepididymal sperm aspiration) requires a narrow needle to be placed into the epididymis to aspirate sperm from this site. This is usually done in cases where the *vas deferens* is blocked or is missing. If both the *vas* and the epididymis are blocked or missing, then sperm may be obtained by placing a biopsy needle into the testes to extract sperm, which may then be microinjected into ova. These three new techniques have demonstrated that even immature and immotile sperm may produce fertilisation and pregnancies, flying in the face of conventional wisdom regarding what makes a viable sperm.

At this point, before concluding the chapter, I must make a plea about ICSI. I helped to pioneer GIFT in the UK (Craft, Lee & Ah-Moye, 1987) and then helped other units to establish GIFT throughout the UK (Davies, Dhariwal & Lee, 1988). In my own experience, GIFT with husband's semen always produced between a 15% and 25% live birth rate. Wherever, I have done GIFT in conjunction with IVF, the GIFT success rate has always been twice that of IVF rates. I do not propose to argue the benefits of GIFT or IVF against each other here. The crux is that in skilled hands, I always expect GIFT to be able to produce 20% live birth rates (even with the most difficult of cases, however not with male factor cases). However once GIFT became a routinely available method in the DGH, GIFT experienced a regression towards the mean, so much so that GIFT is now somewhat passé and national statistics (ILA and HFEA) recently showed GIFT to be a 10% procedure (live birth rates of about 13%, even when donor GIFT results are included). It is possible that ICSI represents a similar situation. In that case I would argue strongly against ICSI being allowed to go the same way as GIFT.

In order to maintain ICSI as a successful treatment option for male infertility, it must be protected and nurtured as a technique (and must yet be subject to a randomised controlled double blind prospective study). The argument for specialised centres of excellence offering ICSI are very strong, otherwise, I fear ICSI will go the way of other new techniques in assisted conception and will be reduced to a 10% procedure or worse, whereby men with male infertility will again be exploited.

Conclusion

I hope it becomes clear that there are few valid treatment options for true male infertility (sperm dysfunction). Over the years, all sorts of methods have been tried. Indeed, some couples have succeeded with treatment, but the success rates have always been less than 5% and there is no clear evidence that the treatment itself was able to give the couples a significantly better chance than they might have had under their own steam (so long as they were still having regular sex). Couples insisting on treatment, particularly GIFT or IVF have always said to me that: yes, they understood the treatments were unlikely to work, but they felt that they must explore all possibilities. They could not accept reaching the end of their reproductive lives and feeling that they did not try everything. The reality is that couples will always open themselves to exploitation when it comes to male infertility, but the truth is that they might be better served if they could only resist the call of the siren and continue to try on their own at home.

The advent of ICSI promises much. We may all hope that it truly represents a breakthrough. I am optimistic to a point. I am almost convinced ICSI is a breakthrough, but regrettably, I am sure it is not a panacea for male infertility. Used in the right way, by those with skills, and for the right patients, I am sure ICSI will become an established method. On the down side, even with careful nurturing, I am sure ICSI will eventually become a 15–20% live birth procedure and will always be provided at a premium price as compared with IVF. Currently ICSI costs in excess of £3000 per cycle. *Caveat emptor!*

Chapter 4
Isolation and Self Punishment

Introduction

At this point, I feel it is relevant to explore the range of emotions that people feel when their expectations and beliefs are challenged by problems in achieving reproduction. I include some of the range of emotions experienced by women, in order to show the similarities and to allow for some comparisons where the emotions may be perceived differently. Much has been written about the female viewpoint (see Corea, 1985; Mahlstedt, 1985; Menning, 1980; Pfeffer & Woollett, 1983; Scutt, 1990), but little about the male viewpoint. Mason (1993) has shed some light on male responses to infertility, but her excellent book consisted of interviews of men rather than containing a counselling perspective. Therefore, there is a paucity of existing literature on men and male infertility, as I have already pointed out in the Introduction to this book. Because of the paucity of information in the literature on men (see also Monach, 1993), I have by necessity had to rely in the main, on my own experiences of working with men.

Bearing the above in mind, it is important to note therefore, the likely limitations of my observations, from which I have found that where crisis and bereavement counselling are common amongst women, men do not come to counselling sessions to work on crisis nor bereavement; Mason (1993) found that all men developed their own methods for survival, but none reported the use of counselling as a coping and survival strategy, rather quoting the uptake of counselling for specific purposes particularly with regard to the stresses of treatment rather than for crisis or bereavement. More on these is discussed later on in this chapter.

The pain of infertility: guilt, blame and loss of self esteem

Koval & Scutt (1990) reported that a social worker suggested that there was an attitude that what all infertile couples needed was a baby, by whatever means! This clearly shows an incomplete understanding of the involuntarily childless and infertile. A more accurate depiction is given by Pfeffer & Woollett (1983) who suggest that among such people, grief is both king and queen. People's (both men and women) own self image of sexual maturity is challenged, leading to a loss of self esteem. The sadness and hurt that such couples feel will fade, but may also easily return according to subsequent life events.

Treatment is a genuine option, just as is the possibility of accepting to 'parent' another child or even utilising one's creativity in other ways. Pfeffer & Wollett (1983) suggest that it is not a good idea to adopt a child (or even to succeed with treatment) until a person has dealt with his or her own negative feelings. They suggest that any hidden or residual resentment might impinge on the parent–child relationship, particularly in adolescence. They go on to describe that for women, there is a type of life crisis (similarly so for men, but men also tend to go into long-term denial). Life centres on the menstrual period, whereby each new period brings about a further chipping away of a woman's self worth. Indeed women may easily feel isolated from the world under these circumstances. The loss of control which seems equally felt by both man and woman is such that there may be significant destruction of a person's identity. Women describe feelings of fear, of feeling so bad that they feel devastated. Obsession about pregnancy is common (Crawshaw, 1995; Jennings, 1995; Scutt (ed.), 1990), and life goes on hold whilst a desperate struggle to produce new life is fought (less common in men).

Koval & Scutt (1990) report that some women have an image of themselves as 'barren' and point out that the burden of guilt is often carried by both male and female. They cite an Australian man, Jeff Smith, who felt it easier to accept infertility since his partner was also branded as infertile. This is commonly reported, apportionment of blame seems to help to adjust the guilt and blame that people feel. Great insight has been given by Smith's description of male role models and expectations in Australia. He suggests that there is a tremendous image of 'the bronzed great lover and great father'. He describes enormous peer pressure to deliver, and to conform to the demands of the role models.

Both man and woman may suffer from the feeling that they are less of a man or woman. Relationships may also easily suffer. Because of the loss of self esteem, both man and woman may feel vulnerable and in need of love and support, which is sadly often lacking because infertility is such a taboo subject. This is particularly so for women since the change in circumstances brings about a change in outlook, so that they become even more isolated and burdened, because friends and family, sensing the awkwardness of the situation become wary, not knowing what to say, or when or how to say anything. An unwanted conspiracy of silence therefore comes about. For men, isolation also comes about, but not for the same reasons. It seems that men are only able to deal with issues of infertility by adopting a macho stance and to turn difficult issues into a joke (Lee, 1995a; Mason, 1993).

Feelings of jealousy and anger are often reported, particularly by women, when observing friends or unknown families in parks, cafés or shops. In terms of the clinics, couples are also required to perform, in other words, to produce sperm and to produce eggs, and then to become pregnant, in order to please the doctors (Scutt (ed.), 1990).

On the other hand, clinics take away a person's feeling of control, which does not help. Couples are scared of showing anger or hurt because they fear the doctors may withdraw treatment. This puts a great deal of pressure on the couples, because they have to perform and also be well behaved. This is further exacerbated by the fact that the vast majority of infertility clinics are attached to the gynaecology clinic, since there are few specialists in male infertility, because few doctors take a specialist interest in the subject (Philipp, 1984).

Furthermore, although many doctors acknowledge that infertility comprises both male and female components, in practice, within the clinics, men are still ignored and marginalised (Bromham *et al.*, 1988; Mason, 1993). Pfeffer & Quick (1988) suggest that part of the problem with the medical profession may lie in their training. Since their training is highly concentrated on diagnosis and treatment, they also tend to ignore the social dimensions of infertility, which in this particular field of medicine may absolutely not be ignored. For instance, patients found that many doctors were particularly insensitive (and lacking in respect and consideration), when dealing with men's diagnosis and prognosis, which led to a great deal of distress and anger (Mason, 1993). Often, doctors would pass on the news at second hand, via the female partner, rather than face the man direct as well as seeming to hide from the gravity of the situation (Snowden *et al.*, 1983). Finally, on the matter of the sociology of the medical profession as pertaining to male infertility, it would appear that male doctors have a particular problem with dealing with infertile men, because of their own beliefs in 'male ideology' (Lee, unpublished observation); worries about homosexuality (Hall, 1991) and because gynaecologists (both male and female) are only used to dealing with reproductive problems of the female (Glover *et al.*, 1990).

Success, and more will be discussed about this later, is not just producing a child. The idea of the womb losing its barrenness or the testes regaining their manhood through success with treatment, belies the possibility that fulfilment for man and woman does not necessarily mean having their own biological child. To continue promoting success with treatment is to perpetuate the cycle of hope, despair and depression. If the couple would only try hard enough, just once more then that miracle might happen.

Bernt, Bernt & Tacke (1992) suggest that men and women behave differently according to the cause of sterility. They suggest that women show higher levels of stress and anxiety in general, irrespective of cause. Interestingly, in all groups, they found that the healthy partner tends to dominate. Subfertile men tend to be more subordinate, less engaged and interested and not so anxious as their wives. Healthy female partners present a highly emotional engagement in overcoming their infertility.

How do men respond to male infertility?

It is interesting to note that an anonymous author has reported that men are reluctant to attend men's groups (Anon, 1994). He also reports continuing reluctance in men to identify themselves. In the same publication, two other articles were also of interest. An article entitled 'The room', by D Rosen (1994) in the summer copy of *Issue* gives a humorous description of what it feels like having to produce a sample in the clinic. (He is lucky – many clinics still make the patient use a lavatory!) In the other article, titled 'Big boys don't cry', Robert Brown (1994), a policeman, describes his personal experience of male infertility (see Fig. 4.1). He reports how men must not cry, particularly in any of the forces. He speaks of being 'outed' and having to deal with it. All the normal euphemisms followed, 'I hear you are firing blanks' said a colleague. Graffiti suddenly appeared on the toilet walls offering him help with 'servicing' his wife. He puts up with it well, looking on it as 'boy's talk', as he puts it. However, infertility strikes at the very core, as he says.

Stress as a factor cannot be underestimated. Indeed Ragni and Caccamo (1992) report that the stress of IVF produced a decline in semen quality in one in eight patients. These results must be tempered by those of Berg, Wilson & Weingartner (1991) who found that gender did not figure significantly, but when considering sex role identification, masculinity was associated with lower strain and greater marital satisfaction when considering infertility. However, the individual set of circumstances must always be considered, since Connolly, Edelmann, Cooke & Robson (1992) also showed that whilst anxiety usually declined from a first visit to a follow up, this was not the case in men who subsequently receive a diagnosis of male infertility. This fact is particularly important when considering DI which circumvents rather than treats the problem of male infertility.

Many women put up with their role of motherhood, which is seen by many men and some women, as being essential components of a woman's marriage as well as her position in society (Crawshaw, 1995; MacCormack, 1980a; Hite, 1991; Ortner, 1974). Within the assisted reproduction scenario, there is the belief that women are more easily able to act as a parent to children of others (Scutt, 1990; Strathern, 1992), though some will usually reject adoption as a solution, partly because of their male partner's disapproval. Many men will express the view that they would prefer to have their own biological child rather than

Joyce

Figure 4.1 *Crying man.* Men with a diagnosis of infertility are 'gutted'. They are wounded to the core. Most men are unable to cry and mourn the shattering of their life's expectations. Having children in both western and many eastern cultures is visual proof of a man's manhood. It is believed that biological parenthood is more important for men than women.

a child genetically not their own (Scutt, 1990). Scutt also (1990) suggests that women, on the other hand, again within the confines of the infertility clinic seem more capable of social motherhood, perhaps one reason why ovum donation is such a popular option for women who have had premature or normal onset menopause, and even for women whose own ovaries are still functioning. The act of being a parent in a social environment is equally as important for them as biological parenthood. However, we should not discount the potential patriarchal influence of their partners (Scutt, 1990), whereby some women will act according to the wishes of their male partners.

However, on the other side of the coin, not all men will wish to pursue treatment. Men faced with DI may elect to remain childless rather than have to become a 'social' parent of their partner's child. Consider Case History 4.1. Particularly when it comes to considering DI treatment, men can be reluctant patients (see also Case History 6.1).

Case history 4.1

Mr and Mrs DD. This couple attended for counselling on the matter of DI. The couple had some disagreements as to how they would progress with treatment. A contract for six sessions was made. Throughout the counselling sessions, Mr DD never moved from his position that he just wanted to get on with his life. To begin with I wondered whether he was just being deliberately obstructive. However, in the end I came to the conclusion that here was a man who knew his own mind. All the explorations we made were always intelligently confronted and any challenges were met with clear reasoned thinking. He had very much enjoyed his childhood, and very much wished to have a child. (However, his thinking relating to kinship was deeply rooted in traditional ways and modern reproduction technology had not changed his way of thinking (Strathern, 1992). The biological aspect of becoming a parent was very important to him.)

At the end of the counselling, Mr DD had not changed his opinion. Whilst Mrs DD attended the sessions, she was present mainly as an interested supporter. Whilst she was happy with the idea of DI, she seemed happy for her partner to explore his feelings and concerns about the treatment option.

The couple in Case History 4.1 are relatively rare. I have seen ten such couples over the years. Often, although the men express reservations, they will eventually consider the treatment. They often express the idea that when they do so, it is a 'gift' to their partner. Even when assenting to DI, they often also freely admit that they still harbour concerns, e.g. they might be worried that they will be unable to be an effective parent to the prospective child or they fear that the child might 'replace' them in their partner's affections. It is also possible that men with no sperm might be more receptive to this form of treatment rather than men with 'poor sperm'.

Snowden & Snowden (1993) have written about DI, suggesting that it is an important part of the infertility specialist's armoury. The title of their book *Gift of a Child* demonstrates their positive viewpoint concerning this type of treatment. They put forward the viewpoint that because there is no past to deal with when DI is used, there is a stronger bond with a child resulting from this treatment than might be the case with adoption. However, they found that in some cases of azoospermia (no sperm in semen sample at all), when DI would be entirely appropriate, paradoxically a group of such men found DI difficult to cope with, as well as finding it hard to come to terms with their infertility.

These issues are reinforced in many ways. With regard to society and children, the legal system works in such a way that women get custody or at least care and control, whereas fathers get access. The inequality of the system further discriminates since men who have access are allowed additional help with taxation. One other area concerns that of dealing with custody, where reasons for refusal of custody to a mother centre on the idea of an 'unfit mother', the paternal equivalent of which does not exist (Crawshaw, 1995). Men lose custody battles because the mother is fit rather than the father being judged as 'unfit'.

In vitro fertilisation for a couple with male factor only is probably unwarranted, but in view of the above, it is possible that many women enter IVF programmes because of their male partner's feelings, fearing rejection by their partners otherwise. Under these circumstances, there is an argument that the female partner, who is healthy and fertile is under coercion from her partner and society in general, to undergo a surgical procedure (with risks), in an attempt to achieve conception (with a relatively low chance of success, at that).

Like many women, men also suffer from low self esteem, loss of self confidence, a feeling of incompetence, a feeling of failure, a feeling of worthlessness, isolation, loneliness, guilt, blame, fear, anger, shame, bitterness and frustration, when they are struggling with male infertility (Lee, 1995a; Mason, 1993). Other feelings expressed by men after they have been given 'a sentence' of male infertility include feeling an outcast and feeling different from everyone else (Mason, 1993). Because of the above and other factors, men, when placed under the spotlight, feel very uncomfortable. Man's right to be supreme is challenged in cases of male infertility, so that not only is the diagnosis a shock, his male ideology as a whole is also challenged. Thus the whole idea of being a man (manhood) is at stake, effectively a man's entire self-belief system is demolished with one blow, thereby placing him in a state of crisis.

Some men are able to rationalise that being infertile does not mean being less human (Lee, 1995a; Mason, 1993), but many do in fact feel that their virility (man's last icon/symbolic role, see Chapter 1) has been called in question, since it is common amongst men to brag about their children and to acknowledge that those who had children had 'proved themselves' (Lee, unpublished observation). One man interviewed by Mason (1993) put things in a nutshell when he said 'we couldn't have a family because of something I couldn't do and that hurts'. Another admitted that rationally he knew that there was no link between fertility and virility, yet when 'you can't do your bit ... I have to put on a brave face with my male friends...'. Many men obviously feel that they have let their partners down.

Because men with children obviously equate parenthood as being an important aspect of manhood, childlessness, especially infertility, is seen by them as an indication of male weakness, which is why most men (and women), including gynaecologists, find it difficult to talk about male infertility (Lee, unpublished observation). In some cases the loss of self confidence and feelings of failure are so strong that a man's work performance will suffer badly. However, some men (probably those stuck in denial) will immerse themselves in their work, working longer and longer hours and seemingly trying to avoid their partners, friends and families (Lee, 1995). Most commonly of all, men feel impotent, sometimes in a sexual way, but more often in a general sense, because they feel so powerless. This type of general impotence leads to massive frustration and anguish because they had always taken this aspect of their future life for granted and now they realise their expectations will not be fulfilled.

In the counselling setting, often the man appears to be detached, remote and uninterested in proceedings (even though in actual fact full of anxiety), because to admit to feelings of distress and to needing help and support goes against male needs for displaying power and control. Conversely, however, the female partner usually attends (in over 90% of cases). It seems that the machismo of the man is under threat. It is often quoted that the link between virility and fertility means that a diagnosis of infertility is a major blow to a man's belief in his own manhood. It is without doubt an important issue, but just how important remains unclear.

Some men have episodes of impotence. Logically, it is probably these men whose virility needs affirmation, whilst the others may not feel their manhood to be under the same threat. It is paradoxical since a few men report the need to increase sexual activity with their partner, because their lack of self esteem leads to a need of confirmation that they are still loved and valued (Mason, 1993), although in one rare case a man needed to bolster his confidence by 'sleeping around' in order to boost his flagging ego (Mason, 1993). However, with regard to sex lives in general, a few reported no change or an improvement (because of increased spontaneity since contraception was no longer needed?), but most men report reduced activity, mainly because they felt like and expressed the following metaphors: 'feel like a performing seal', 'seemed pointless making love', 'things had become mechanical' and 'the pleasure had gone from sex' (Lee, 1995a; Mason, 1993).

Putting aside the feelings relating to loss of potency, men also often experience a feeling of guilt, blame and a sense of uselessness begins to surface. Indeed, in many cultures, a man's ability to have offspring is linked to his social standing and potency. Confirmation of male factor (sperm dysfunction), brings all these emotions to a head. Indeed, crisis, a powerful feeling of shock and panic are key emotions.

Crisis is an important aspect of counselling in infertility. As mentioned in the Introduction, this is not a comprehensive 'how to do it' book and those looking for more about this specialised discipline should read Janosik (1984) and Parry (1990). Furthermore, my experience of counselling men for crisis is rare (see also Mason, 1993), although women commonly request crisis counselling. Somehow men bottle up their feelings and seek to cope with their crisis in any number of ways (for example, denial, crying in private, enduring solitary sadness and depression, immersing oneself in work, playing more sport etc). The pain, confusion and agony of the diagnosis are thus endured silently, because of the fear that others will find out and view them as being less of men (Lee, 1995a; Mason, 1993). Mahlstedt (1985) and Menning (1980) have written specifically about crisis and bereavement within the infertility setting. Recognising crisis (Ayalon, 1990; Parry, 1990; Mahlstedt, 1985; Menning, 1980), which occurs commonly amongst both male and female infertility patients, involves looking for situations where the client's belief system or a life goal may have been challenged or blocked (i.e. belief and expectation of parenthood), where there might be a problem which seems insoluble in the immediate future especially where a shock has occurred, a situation where existing resources and traditional problem-solving methods are overtaxed; all these above possibilities are compounded with their denial, anger and guilt and often, although grief is a key issue that needs to be worked with, the bereavement process is left in limbo.

Other observations include those of Parry (1990) who suggests watching out for loss of sleep and/or appetite, anxiety and depression, recent development of problems with reasoning or decision making and recent development of severe aches and pains or intense anger, guilt and shame. Egan (1990) suggests that dealing with crisis involves looking for appropriate leverage points (identifying the root of the crisis) and initially slowly working on aspects of the problem which are easiest to deal with, which will bring about immediate improvement in the person's condition.

Parry (1990) has provided an excellent checklist in her book and also describes the importance of managing stress (in particular relaxation therapy; see also O'Moore, 1986) and helping to contain the client's crisis. Dealing with depression is an important part of managing crisis which has been mentioned by all the aforementioned authors. Indeed all of us working in the field of infertility must learn to acknowledge these emotions in our clients and patients and to develop the skills we need to help them deal with them. It is important to develop our resources as well as recognising our own limitations and knowing when to refer to outside agencies and specialists.

These emotions may persist for years. In women, one emotion which may persist for many years is that of denial and a feeling of loss. The bereavement aspect is very important for women (Crawshaw, 1995;

Jennings, 1995) and may last for many years. For men, this feeling of bereavement does not seem to be so important, although, it is likely that this is due to total denial (Lee, unpublished observation), but there is insufficient research data available yet to be sure. Mason (1993), however, found that only five out of the 22 men that she interviewed had significant things to say about loss and bereavement of the prospective child.

Jennings (1995) points out that grieving for a child that has never existed is a peculiar situation (often protracted) made unique by reproduction technology and is therefore a good example of the type of displacement that Strathern (1992) talks about. Certainly, when dealing with bereavement in this setting, we need to understand the uniqueness of the situation and to find ways in which each individual may ritualise (Jennings, 1995) such as the 'passing of their dream child(ren)'. Cabau & de Senarclens (1986), Mahlstedt (1985) and Menning (1980) have all stressed the importance of the bereavement process for patients with infertility. Mahlstedt (1985) suggests that patients are faced with all the losses that characteristically cause clinical depression.

All the authors cited above have expressed the belief that infertility is a life crisis in which grief is an important emotion. By grieving their losses, patients may be able to move on and thereby benefit more from their treatment or indeed in rare cases of resolution to get on with their childless lives. Bor & Scher (1995) have suggested various ways of preparing clients for loss. It is important to explore the meaning of loss and mourning with the client and its relationship to the future. In particular the healing power of time itself is also an important element. Ayalon (1990) feels that myth and ritual are important aspects of counselling in bereavement. Like Jennings (1995) he believes that metaphor is a powerful way of dealing with such emotional and painful issues. An example of how visualisation may be used in the course of bereavement work is given in Chapter 6.

In my experience, men seem to work with the feeling of guilt and uselessness as the key long-term emotions. Anger is also prevalent, although it will usually be denied at first. The anger is not always explicit, nor necessarily present at home, but is more easily displayed at work. Often the anger is released over issues unrelated to infertility, but over any irritating issue, particularly at work. A key word which is often unspoken is *frustration*. Because of the overwhelming tendency of men to deny their plight, there is an irrevocable commitment to isolation, which is the main feeling shared by all Mason's interviewees. This self-isolation makes men particularly difficult to deal with both from a medical aspect as well as a counselling aspect. The isolation results in tremendous feelings of loneliness (many men feel they are unique and alone), and is further exacerbated by friends and family beginning to avoid them as they themselves feel guilty when they realise how distressed infertile persons and couples are. Isolation is therefore compounded by this conspiracy of silence. This veil of secrecy also exists because men themselves are too embarrassed to bring the subject of infertility up amongst their peers because of the association of sex and sexuality with infertility and furthermore to admit to a need to talk about the issue is an admission of weakness.

Men demonstrate an overriding need to know why (Lee, 1995; Mason, 1993). Where there are no sperm, men face the most powerful immediate reactions to the diagnosis, but may find it easier to accept their plight than otherwise (Lee, unpublished observation; Mason, 1993), however, when there are some sperm present in the semen sample, these men need considerably longer to come to terms with their issues. Moreover, men with congenital problems (problems arising from defects present at birth) also seemed to feel less guilt and anxiety, presumably because they are therefore blameless, whilst those with idiopathic 'poor sperm' and those whose infertility was ascribed to overindulgence in drugs, alcohol and cigarette smoking seemed to suffer more anguish from guilt and anxiety. Indeed, some clients find it hard to understand how they are infertile when they still have sperm. Thus they grapple with the problem, often continuing for years to pursue treatments.

The more technology moves on, the harder it is for patients like this to accept their diagnosis and to resolve their feelings about their infertility. It is probably this group of men who are more prone to lower self esteem and clinical depression. Without doubt the pursuit of treatment is for some patients an act of denial. Although crisis and bereavement work is rare with men in the counselling setting, they must of course find some way of coping with, if not undergoing resolution of crisis and loss. It would seem that time is the greatest healer for them as well as trying to find a reason for their plight. In my own experience, I find I am often placed in the role of information giver in respect of the 'whys' that such clients come with to counselling sessions.

Thus we can see that both men and women often arrive at the same place, but for different reasons. We have not yet dealt in detail with the loss of self esteem. This is undoubtedly common and is always readily acknowledged. The man many deny anger, deny feelings of loss of virility/potency, but he will almost always be willing to disclose a loss of self esteem. Yet it is in my experience so very difficult to explore these feelings with men. Sometimes denial is so complete that the man will just immerse himself in his work, refusing to accept the diagnosis, even refusing to attend the clinic any further or carrying out acts of sabotage (e.g. too busy to attend, being unable to produce a semen sample). Case History 4.2 is unusual, insofar that although it is really about a man, it comes from the viewpoint of a woman.

Case history 4.2

Mrs F came for counselling and was at her wits end. Her husband had been told that he had a low sperm count and since then had refused to go back to the infertility clinic. No matter what she did, she could not per-suade him to acknowledge the problem. He completely denied the situation and in fact started to spend more and more time at work. He kept telling her that 'it would happen' naturally and that they should not worry. Mr F took to working very long and unpredictable hours. On occasions, after arguments, he would even walk out. He was a very successful businessman and infertility just did not fit in with his lifestyle nor life plans. He kept telling his wife that they had a lovely life and that they had so many options. They could even go to Hong Kong and lead a lovely 'expatriate' life for a few years if she wanted to. He did not see any need to panic or do anything yet. During the six sessions, it became obvious that the denial was bringing Mr and Mrs F perilously close to separation. Mr F never attended.

When I last enquired (up to three years later) the couple had not had any treatment and have subsequently been lost to follow up. My feeling is that they did indeed separate. Such decisions are not that rare within the infertility clinic setting.

Summary about men's feelings

For all men who are told that they have male infertility, there are immediately a number of issues which might be dealt with. There are not necessarily any number of consistent themes, since different per-sons will perceive different issues as being vital ones (see also Mason, 1993). There is often a link between fertility and someone's manhood (macho element). They are also often private persons, with a few extrovert exceptions. Anger is overt only in rare cases, where the male partner is spoiling for a fight, which is projected as being on behalf of his partner, for example, and rarely acknowledged as belonging to himself.

The diagnosis of male subfertility is a big blow to a person's self esteem. In some, even in cases of azoospermia, there is complete denial. Often, they will ask 'why me?' It is almost as if the answer to this question will in some way salve the pain. They will often complain that other less deserving people have children, and it seems a gross injustice that they cannot. Inevitably there are also issues over the apportionment of blame. It is common for the female partner to express relief and a shifting of burden when the spotlight falls on the male partner. There exists also the issues of 'is God punishing me?' and 'what have I done to deserve this?' A common summation of all these feelings, especially within the medical setting, is a growing feeling of total uselessness. There seems so little that can be done for male infertility. Any treatment options seem to centre almost entirely on the blameless partner (the female). This results in the man feeling marginalised. When looking at cultural differences, there is an added emotional charge, for example Middle Eastern men often cannot accept that they are the cause of the infertility.

Guilt and punishment

I cannot end this chapter without exploring the issue of guilt and punishment a little further. Issues of guilt and punishment seem common, particularly among women. Men and women report often on situations where they observe others with children. They see children treated badly or hear people state that they wished they did not have their children. The women report feeling bad and sad that they themselves who wish so much for children, are unable to. Life seems so unfair. These people who seem so undeserving, yet have children, make it appear to the infertile and the childless that they must be bad people since they do not have the children they long for. If people who are so undeserving are allowed to have children, and they are not, they take on board the idea that they must themselves be very undeserving. A consequence of these feelings is to lose further self esteem, and to ingest an enormous amount of guilt and to believe that somehow they have been so evil some time in their lives that they are being punished for being undeserving. The story of one such couple is outlined in Case History 4.3.

Case history 4.3

Mr and Mrs H were agonising over their IVF treatment. A contract for six sessions was agreed on. During counselling it became clear that there were a number of issues involved. They were both teachers and found the stress of the job considerable. They had had one attempt at IVF and found the idea of another one a harrowing prospect. Mr H also had a low sperm count, but had stopped smoking and drinking and tried, in general, to adopt a positive outlook.

Because the couple were teachers, we explored the issue of ambivalence, both from the female and the male point of view (see Chapter 5). Mr and Mrs H felt that it was likely that ambivalence did play a role in their anxieties. Looking to the IVF, both seemed to be very negative about the next treatment attempt. They seemed almost willing to 'run away'. When exploring the issues relating to the anxiety concerning the IVF, we chanced upon the guilt and punishment. This became the focus of the third session. During this session, it seemed that Mrs H viewed her own womb as a derelict place, a place where nothing would grow (a common metaphor, see Jennings, 1995). It was a dark place. Both

Case history 4.3 *continued*

Mr and Mrs H possessed a rich vein of metaphors in their language (see Lee, 1995a; Jennings, 1995), and also seemed highly receptive to visualisation exercises. Working through the medium of visualisation we began to explore Mrs H's barren land. Homework for Mrs H at the end of the third session consisted of doing a painting of her womb (see Campbell, 1995).

Mrs H brought her painting to session four. This session concentrated on the painting. We looked, we discussed, and we contemplated. Towards the end of the session, we began to work with the theme of seeing things begin to grow in the barren land.

In session five, Mrs H arrived looking fresh and bright. Mr H was also very vibrant. Mr H announced that he felt very very positive now. Mrs H felt that she had made a major breakthrough regarding her barren womb. She had been carrying out her visualisation exercises and could now see it being a place where things might grow. At the end of this session, we returned to the theme of guilt and punishment. Almost intuitively, Mr and Mrs H saw that the time had come for them to give themselves permission to have children. Indeed, for Mrs H, the fertile womb indicated she had already reached this state. She only needed to verbalise it in order truly to own it. Armed with this, they went away in a positive frame of mind.

The sixth session took place when they should have been having treatment. Alas, the cycle had to be abandoned because of a poor response to ovarian stimulation. Nevertheless, the couple welcomed the opportunity for support. They still felt the treatment process was stressful. Nevertheless, in spite of the abandonment, they still seemed in an upbeat mood. The session ended with Mr and Mrs H earnestly requesting further support if need be in the future. I assured them my door would not be closed. At the time of writing, some 12 months on, I have not heard from them yet.

This issue of guilt and punishment is so strong that, even if the male does not feel it himself, the idea is assimilated as affecting a couple. The ultimate consequence of all of this is that, in a strange way, the couple seem to begin subconsciously to see treatment (especially where it is private) as the only means of obtaining a baby. In a way, this is ultimately the modern equivalent of the medieval method of buying absolution (the buying of indulgences which was meant to excuse the buyer from several thousand years of purgatory prior to Judgement day). In religious parlance, this meant that religious forgiveness could be obtained from the church by the payment of money; the more you paid, the more you were let off.

Conclusion

Clearly, men's responses to male infertility mirror those of women. Reasons for the responses differ slightly though, and certainly depend on individual circumstances as well. For men, key issues seem to be denial, loss of self esteem, marginalisation and isolation. Crisis is also common in both male and female, though where women readily seek help for this, men avoid this issue and bury themselves deep in isolation, because to seek help is to deny one's manliness. Since male infertility has already undermined the man's foundations, to seek counselling help for his crisis situation might be the final straw.

Bereavement does not seem to be a factor for men, perhaps mainly because men are stuck in denial and are therefore unable to move on in order to resolve feelings of bereavement. I asked one client of mine, who freely agreed that he was stuck in denial, whether he thought he might end his days as a childless person; gnarled, bitter and lonely. His partner quickly piped up that she thought this was currently his life's ambition.

With regard to the idea of guilt, punishment and indulgences, the longer I work in this field, the more I am convinced that men and women reinforce their own belief in their infertility through the issues of guilt and punishment. Ultimately, they must either find forgiveness in themselves or pay for their indulgences, in order to finally give themselves permission to have the children they so strongly desire.

Chapter 5
Coping and Coming to Terms with Male Infertility

Introduction

We have thus far looked at the following: the concept of crisis in man, diagnosis of male infertility, treatment options and the themes of guilt and punishment. In this chapter we look further in depth at men, how they think, how they feel about and respond to their infertility, and how in general terms they may be given support. More detailed analysis on counselling men is given in the next chapter.

Dealing with infertile men: what can be done for them?

Because of their responses to diagnosis, few men seek help. Most will suffer in silence since male ideology dictates that men don't cry, and that when the going gets tough, the tough get going. Men deal with their own problems, men do not need help from anyone else. Consequently, it is rare to arrive in the counselling setting at situations which are initiated by men. Mason (1993) found that there was a general reluctance amongst most of her interviewees and that where some had taken up counselling, they had not found it particularly useful. When men attend for sessions, it is usually as a result of a mandatory referral (no further treatment until...) arising from a label of difficult or angry patient. Otherwise, in their own minds, they are present in order to support their partner rather than for themselves. Furthermore, even more taboo, in my experience, is the fact that men do not like group sessions, as stated by the anonymous author in Chapter 4.

Much of working with men therefore depends on working on the principle of providing counselling through the art of 'counselling without counselling', i.e. counselling which is offered in a non-counselling environment. Often the men arrive in such circumstances by the subterfuge of their partners (see Case History 5.1). For me, much of my counselling has been done within the confines of consultations for male infertility. Overtly the men come willingly for consultation. Then within the setting of a consultation, when given the possibility of exploring their plight in a less/non threatening scenario, most men are able freely to explore issues relating to their own experience of male infertility. This works to such an extent that I now routinely put aside one hour for these consultations. If I were to allow three hours, most patients would take it up.

Case history 5.1

Mr and Mrs R attended a male infertility workshop. During the workshop, Mrs R announced that Mr R was only there because she had told him that he was coming to a cheese and wine party at the clinic. During the workshop, Mrs R had been an active participant. Although Mr R had been very quiet, he volunteered that he had found it all very useful and interesting, in spite of his initial reluctance.

This case serves to illustrate how shy men are about counselling. Indeed as mentioned in the previous paragraph, men are even more reluctant to attend group therapy, but may be persuaded to attend workshops and information or advice giving sessions.

However the sessions arise, whether overt or covert, I feel it is important to explore men's feelings of anguish in detail. There are no real answers to the 'why me?' and the 'what have I done to deserve it?' questions, but in my experience it has been useful to affirm the absurdity of life; in other words to acknowledge the unfairness of the situation. It may be useful to challenge the client's feelings of guilt and uselessness. It may be helpful to explore ways of bolstering their self esteem and marshalling their own resources (one hopes these are substantial). In exploring men's potential resources as regards their male friends, it seems that this is rarely an option. Whenever any of my clients have tried to share their secrets, the response from male friends is usually to make a joke of it or to trivialise it. Everyone always has an apocryphal tale to tell. A common response is to offer to help out with the wife (see Chapter 4). Sometimes there is embarrassed silence, then it is swept under the carpet and the matter becomes taboo (the veil of silence descends).

As a consequence of the above, men often report that they are very hurt. They have a sense that the whole world knows about their plight and is laughing at them. They often exclaim resentment and bitterness; that they are 'jaffas' (i.e. seedless), or that they have been 'firing blanks'. Many find it ironic that they have spent years worrying about contraception. There is little that I have ever found of use to say, when men report these feelings of hurt. It seems enough just to listen sympathetically. Sometimes I have found it useful, when counselling the strong silent type, to ask them about their experience of the above, as a means of engaging them.

Many share a type of depression, and seem to experience a quiet desperation. It is not easy being a genetic cul-de-sac. I often ask depressed clients how they view the future. 'Do they see themselves being old, childless and bitter?' (one wife gave an answer which I found both touching and in the absurdity of the moment quite funny, see end of Chapter 4). It is certainly useful to determine how their fantasies of the future manifest. In many men there is an heroic type of self sacrifice. Some volunteer immediately for DI and seemingly have all the right things to say. This reaction does not mean that shock, disbelief and frustration aren't present, but somehow, in a paradoxical type of denial, they seek too quickly to resolve their anxieties.

Many men have reported such feelings mentioned above (see also Chapter 4); it seems that the absurdity of being 'seedless' and the callous reactions of their work mates and friends leave them feeling bitter and isolated. The following case histories (5.2a,b,c) are snapshots of some of the responses men have made over the years. The first one is very representative. The second one obviously has cultural aspects to it (see Chapter 8), whilst the third one shows that there are also men whose thinking is on another planet.

Case history 5.2a

Mr OD was very depressed. His infertility was long-standing (11 years). He obviously felt that many of the years had been wasted by too many tests and inappropriate treatment. He found it hard to sleep and was becoming increasingly frustrated. He felt that his marriage was under imminent threat. He found it very hard to accept that the cause for the infertility lay at his door, though he did exclaim on a number of occasions that he was a 'jaffa' with a great deal of bitterness. He worked in a hospital and had friends who were nurses. In spite of the professional background of his male colleagues, he also experienced some cruel comments and suggestions.

Case history 5.2b

Mr NO was a Nigerian businessman. When told of his infertility, he looked somewhat upset and a little puzzled. After an IVF attempt which produced no fertilisation, Mr and Mrs NO seemed to take the news reasonably well. Some hours afterwards, I found Mr NO waiting to see me in the waiting room. He had waited there most patiently and quietly. He seemed very apologetic. Eventually, he worked round to the IVF failure and pointed out to me that he was very puzzled, the reason being that only last year he had impregnated a sixteen year old virgin, so how could it be that he was infertile now?

Case history 5.2b *continued*

I had to think hard about this one. Not knowing about the cultural aspects and in my ignorance at the time, not thinking of asking him to enlighten me, I took the coward's way out and suggested to him that there were two possibilities. (1) he had experienced a sudden disastrous loss in fertility, which might only be temporary, or (2) the IVF failure might possibly be related to egg factors. I must confess, that ever since, whenever I am faced by a similar set of circumstances, although I hope I am more capable of determining the cultural background to such issues, I cannot help but think of Mr NO and his 'sixteen year old pregnant virgin test of male infertility'.

Case history 5.2c

This is a short case history involving Mr A, B, C, D..., although I must admit, I have only been asked this about ten times in my career. Nevertheless, under the circumstances, I must admit to being flabbergasted by men who have said the following to me after being given their diagnosis: 'You mean that after all these years of taking precautions I haven't needed to? So, when I am with my lover/mistress, is it now safe to have sex without taking precautions?

What can I say? I usually say no. Just because a person is experiencing infertility with one partner does not guarantee the same with another.

Male infertility and episodes of impotence

Some men find that they begin to have problems with sex, because somehow it loses meaning when it does not produce the desired child. With regard to male infertility, up to 25% of couples may intermittently be in this strange state of celibacy outside treatment, particularly the men who feel that virility is linked to their ability to father a child, although some men report no changes in their libido. In my experience long-term impotence is rare, although periodic impotence seems to be a side effect of male infertility, usually arising at the worst point in a man's experience. For instance, when he is told that nothing more can be done, or the only way forward is to consider DI. For those who feel that sex has become mechanical or in its extreme form, for those who become impotent, I have found it useful to affirm the man's feelings. Some psychosexual counselling may be required to deal with impotence. Reassurance followed by an exploration of what the man feels might put him at ease and is useful. Further exploration of other strategies (more relaxation, going out as a couple for a meal or to the cinema, focusing less on the penetration aspect of sex for a while, etc.) may also be helpful. The main goal is to try to reassign sex with its many priorities in life and so put the reproduction aspect into its true perspective. Often the couple are also in a rut. Exploration of family life often reveals boring routine and the loss of spontaneity and sparkle. Goal setting in the way of 'doing something different', perhaps simply re-establishing the idea of cuddling may be useful in dealing with impotence. Deep seated impotence will require outside referral to a sex therapist or urologist (if surgery is needed). Impotence has also been discussed in Chapters 2 and 3.

Sensate focus has already been outlined in Chapter 3. Below is a collection of exercises which specifically relate to overcoming psychologically based impotence, and incorporate the method of sensate focus.

Impotence

Exercise 1. No sex at this stage. Massage of non-genital areas only.

Exercise 2. Still no sex, but massage of genital areas now allowed. First, the male partner should gently stimulate his partner's clitoris. Orgasm is not mandatory.

Exercise 3. The female partner now takes up the lead role. An erection is not important at this stage. The male partner should relax and simply enjoy being stroked and fondled. The female partner should alternate between the stroking and stopping. This teasing should encourage the penis to respond when stimulated. If an erection occurs, stimulation to ejaculation is allowed, but still no sex until confidence has been built up.

Exercise 4. Repeat exercise 3. Books or videos may also enhance the experience. (Oral sex is allowed at this stage.)

Exercise 5. At this point, sex is allowed. A good position is to allow the woman on top. If the erection is lost on penetration, the couple should rest, perhaps look at some books or a video and then start again. The couple should try to relax and simply enjoy the feelings and sensations of the exercises.

At any stage it may be appropriate to go back rather than forward. All couples should proceed at their own pace.

Marie-Claire Mason (1993) wrote an important chapter titled 'The desire to be a father', where she looked at men's need to be a father. Some men wanted to improve their own experience, some wanted to prove themselves to the rest of the world, some just wanted to have children. The idea of not being able to seemed to play a strong role in the resultant desire, which is then paradoxically heightened. Then the striving and the failure somehow seems to feed on the growing yearning for a child. One man described how his yearnings involved fantasies about what he would do with his child. His pain was made worse when he saw other fathers realising his fantasies. There were also aspects of property and ownership for some men. One man resented the fact that he would be unable to pass on the benefit of his life experiences to any children. The idea of passing things on and, in a way, becoming immortal through having offspring is deep seated in mankind's kinship systems (see MacCormack & Strathern (eds.), 1980). Many men reported the feeling of resentment that those lucky enough to have children seemed to take them for granted and did not cherish them as they themselves imagined they would. Some felt even more strongly, not just about experience but also regretted the inability to pass on their family characteristics. Here there may well be issues of competitiveness with siblings who had succeeded in procreation.

Life seems senseless and some men feel that without children they are unable to take up their position fully within the ranks of men. Such rites of passage into manhood are not universal, but common enough (MacCormack & Strathern (eds.), 1980; Strathern, 1992). Indeed, Jennings (1995) has shown that the Temiar people of southeast Asia do not exclude from adulthood persons who are infertile. They simply become 'parents of no children'. The idea of parenting as opposed to fatherhood may be a positive way of dealing with issues of fatherhood, and as reproduction technology moves on bringing with it novel kinship ideas, the image of 'biological' father may be replaced by that of 'sociological father' (Strathern, 1992). It seemed clear to Mason that there were indeed aspects of ambivalence in all the men she interviewed.

Dealing with ambivalence

Fatherhood may provide some men with a chance to care for children and to experience feelings they would otherwise not have. They might also be able to understand their own childhood better and if necessary relive and put to rights any defects in their own upbringing (Mason, 1993). Fatherhood also gives a person a sense of the passing of generations, for example it is a rite of passage that is so important in life (already considered in Chapter 1). Men may be reluctant to admit the above because male ideology means that work and power are the things men should be worried about primarily rather than issues of fertility. Furthermore, men have access to many more roles than women (Crawshaw, 1995; Monach, 1993). Many men with children certainly demonstrate this, whereby their work outside the family is number one and family life is clearly in a distant second place.

Ambivalence is an important issue, for both men and women (Lee,

1995a). In the context of male infertility, we are examining an area where men have hidden agendas. Perhaps there is a fear of growing up, establishing stable relationships with *responsibility*. There may be history of abuse in childhood. Most importantly, we should bear in mind that it is not just the physical that may affect a person's fertility. There is the real likelihood that for so-called unexplained infertility and some cases of male infertility, that ambivalence may be a major issue. Here it is possible that intervention with counselling or related therapy might be as useful as conventional infertility treatments.

Psychogenic infertility

This is a contentious issue. Clearly, in the section on ambivalence (and in other chapters where I have described certain case histories), I am making a clear allusion to the possibility that the subconscious mind may be able to affect a person's fertility (Lee, 1995a; Wheeler, 1994). Whilst the idea is fairly well documented (Harrison, 1986; Kemeter, 1990; O'Moore, 1986; Palti, 1969; Rubinstein, 1951; Sandler, 1968), most specialists are unwilling to accept the existence of the subconscious mind having an influence on fertility. Furthermore, it is important to stress that whilst some of us who work in the field have clearly observed instances of so-called psychogenic infertility, we see a clear distinction between this and what some people have described as the 'infertile personality' which is an unfortunate turn of phrase as it attempts to pathologise matters in a way which is not helpful.

A comprehensive review on the matter has been written by Cabau & de Senarclens (1986). They conclude that further study on the contribution of psychology to infertility is warranted, nevertheless even after an extensive literature search they were unable to determine the physiological basis. For instance, it might be argued that stress and anxiety might affect prolactin levels which may in turn affect a person's fertility. However, the link between stress and a direct effect on a person's gonadotrophin levels remains to be determined.

Accepting childlessness

Treatment is not always the right course of action. Sometimes, acceptance is a very powerful emotion. Being able to acknowledge one's fears and to face up to them may help some couples to make decisions which allow them to control their own destinies (Jennings, 1995; Lee, 1995a), but, as Mason (1993) points out, it is a complex process, which perhaps few manage to complete. Strathern (1992) has shown that because technology produces new possibilities, couples may never catch up with the technology, so they will continue to hope and desire without the containment of time boundaries; egg donation, surrogacy, DI and IVF conspire to make desire and hope a moving feast. Treatment is not always essential. Being challenged over the possibility of accepting childlessness is a worthwhile exercise. In my own work, the ability to accept childlessness is less common amongst men who have sperm in their semen (no matter how few). These men seem to be driven to persist with treatment and will continue to hang on to the slightest thread of hope. The group in which I have found the highest rate of acceptance of childlessness is that of those who have azoospermia and who, for whatever reason, have chosen not to consider DI. Below is a case history of one such client.

Case history 5.3

Mr B is a business professional from an upper middle class English background. He has azoospermia. His partner is keen to press on with DI treatment, but he is unwilling. During exploration about his plight, Mr B revealed a range of emotions and anxieties consistent with a man who has been diagnosed as azoospermic as a consequence of primary testicular failure. He was clearly wounded to the core by his condition and clearly bitterly resented the idea of being a genetic cul-de-sac. Tears welled in his eyes as we considered his fantasies about the children he would never have. His replies to questions indicated that he was on the path of working through bereavement (accepting the loss of the fantasy children).

He would not participate in DI, reporting that for him it was very important to bring up children of his own. The idea of being a social parent did not appeal at all. I challenged Mr B a great deal about these feelings and explored the feelings of his wife and her possible response to his decision. At the end of the day, he affirmed his need to accept childlessness and was articulate about the benefits of this point of view.

Sources of support

Family may sometimes be a source of support. Parents may on occasions be supportive. More often it seems that the mother is the better source of succour (as almost always); fathers often being silent (where have we seen this before?). Often, because there is tremendous parental pressure on the issue of grandchildren, help from this quarter is not sought. Sometimes, especially in cases of male infertility, parents may harbour guilt and blame, often wishing they had done something for their son earlier. Thus parents can often enter into the conspiracy of silence that many couples face.

Brothers and sisters may also be a good source of support. In cases involving male infertility, siblings may often be the best resource available. Friends, male friends in particular, are particularly insensitive and unhelpful. Most men who have trusted or confided in male friends have ended up regretting their actions. The situation with work colleagues being similar. In these circumstances, the men found themselves the butt of their workmates' jokes.

Perhaps, at the end of the day, a couple's best resource is themselves (see also Lee, 1995a; Mason, 1993). I have started to point this out with couples when goal setting. Each must support the other. Because the conspiracy of silence can be so very strong in cases of male infertility, the couple themselves are their own greatest resource. In this way, the couple's relationship may benefit from their sorrow. Fortunately, most women are well suited to the role. Whether their partners are equally good at reciprocating is another matter.

Male ideology, manhood and men's need to control

Male fertility is a symbol of sexual potency (Hite, 1991). The threat to a man's potency is a threat to his identity, which renders him powerless. Thus a man feels that his ability to control the world he lives in is also threatened. Men feel a tremendous need to be active and in control. Thus in the clinic where the medical specialist, usually a gynaecologist, is all powerful, the man is reduced to the role of flapping around help-lessly, trying desperately to exert some control, but the clinic makes all the decisions, rendering the man ineffectual (isolated and marginalised) and impotent (Humm, 1989). Consequently there is no apparent role for the man. The men try to sort out treatment and to get information, but they are rendered sterile at every turn. The clinic and the staff effectively emasculate them too (Mason, 1993). During counselling therefore, the issue of male ideology and control is well worthwhile exploring. It may then be useful to look at various strategies and goals which might help men to deal with these feelings when confronted by them.

Men like autonomy, so scheduled sex further robs a man of inde-pendence and renders him powerless. Men make decisions with their heads, always rationalising. Thus infertility demonstrates one thing above all else; that the drive to have children owes little to reason; no wonder men become disoriented. For men this disorientation leads to crisis, which arises, because they have no clear role, even though they have the infertility and not their partners. A man must try to cope with his feelings, yet his upbringing makes this difficult to do, he feels guilty and useless (Lee, 1995a). Many men then focus their energies on work, which may cause the relationship to suffer (see Case History 4.2). This results in many men refusing to acknowledge issues and being reluctant to be open about sex, which as mentioned before may sometimes end up in them having episodes of impotence.

Men are often unaware of their own emotional needs, and even when they are, seem incapable of demanding that they be addressed (Lee, 1995a). Clearly, for the vast majority of men, infertility has strongly challenged their expectancies of life. Most men report that they had always expected to one day have children. Diagnosis of male infertility is not just a shock therefore, but clearly an issue of major crisis (Lee, 1995a; Mason, 1993; Mahlstedt, 1985; Menning, 1980). All men affected desperately want to regain some form of control. Almost always the first port of call is to seek medical help. Some are able to examine the possibility of childlessness in the long term, and in so doing are also able to look at their lives and at the possibility of opening a new chapter in their story book. Regrettably, in my travels I have rarely found a man who is capable of positively reappraising his life effectively whilst he is still held thrall by uncertainties in his life. Thus, if he and/or his partner continue to seek medical help, trailing from clinic to clinic, the record certainly seems to get stuck; and there is a great difference in the man who immerses himself in work and one who has come to terms with childlessness and is then able to take up new interests, whether work or otherwise. In counselling, when I come across such clients, I try to challenge their vision of their situation, pointing out that they may be in a rut and that they might benefit from writing a new story for themselves. Many will almost certainly benefit from 'moving on'.

In her book, when looking at coping strategies, Marie-Claire Mason (1993) refers to Stanton (1991) who outlines the following coping strategies:

- Confrontational – fighting for what is desired
- Distancing – denial
- Self-control – keeping feelings internalised
- Seeking support
- Accepting responsibility – I brought the problem on myself (not relevant in male infertility)
- Escape/avoidance – hoping for miracle
- Problem solving
- Positive reappraisal.

Mason suggests that men usually seem to adopt the second and third strategies. Some will fight, some will hope for a miracle (hope is a frightening quantity). A few may seek support from those other than their partner, with mainly bad experiences to report. A few will reappraise their lives. I mentioned earlier in this chapter and in the previous chapter that men get stuck in denial, therefore, grief counselling is an important part of our work, but can one initiate it? Unfortunately positive reappraisal may not be possible until we have worked through the above.

Conclusion

Men are generally reluctant to consider support let alone formal support such as counselling. Men seem to want to cope on their own, resenting intrusion. Furthermore those who have been counselled do not seem to appreciate the process. Men do not like the idea of support groups and are wary. They do however seem to like newsletters, but are clearly worried in general about coercion to have counselling or to go to support group meetings, probably because any of these actions implies even more loss of control for them, when they are already feeling impotent (not physically). Thus, we need to look at how we may address these very real fears that men have and to encourage them to seek support and to take the opportunity of being counselled without being threatened. There is much to be done from the point of education.

In dealing with men, perhaps we need to look much harder at the issues of loss and mourning, otherwise there is a strong likelihood that many men will be unable to move on, perhaps never coming to terms with their infertility. The pain may then never diminish or go away. The uncertainty and our lack of understanding make it harder to achieve resolution in men. This makes it harder to work through grief and loss, especially when men with sperm are unable to give up their hold on hope; it really is a *Catch 22* situation. For men with azoospermia, the situation may often be a little simpler.

Chapter 6
Counselling Men: Summarising Current Understanding and Exploring What Needs to be Done

Introduction

A number of the female partners of patients have reported to me that it was a relief eventually to find that the fault lay with their husband and not them. This serves to demonstrate the pressures on a person to avoid blame. To be the cause of a couple's infertility is to assume the mantle of enormous pressure. For men (bear in mind they have already been portrayed as the neglected patient in infertility clinics, as well as being burdened by the shackles of male ideology), the idea of being the partner with the 'problem' seems to place a tremendous burden on the individual (Lee, 1995a; Mason, 1993). They feel blame very strongly and assume a strong sense of guilt. For men, particularly those in Europe and the USA, because men don't cry and that they somehow manage all types of life disasters by 'toughing it out' (Hite, 1991; Lee, 1995a; Mason, 1993), infertility is a bitter pill. Men seem in general to be unable to seek help, particularly those steeped in male ideology (see Chapters 1, 4, 5 and 7), who face immense pressures as they strive to maintain a public face, whilst inwardly, their very fabric has been almost fatally shredded.

Some men never come to terms with their infertility. Technology makes it even harder, because their desires are fired by the hope that someone will find a solution, which is just round the next corner (Jennings, 1995; Mason, 1993; Strathern, 1992). On the other hand, particularly when considering DI, some men arrive at acceptance too readily (see Chapter 9, Lee 1995a; Mason, 1993), which might indicate denial and could mean problems arising at a future date. In the main, most men achieve a type of balance, whereby they learn to live with the pain, which however makes them more susceptible to severe stress and life crisis. Unfortunately men cannot find it in themselves to seek help (Greenstein, 1993; Lee, 1995a; Monach, 1993; Mason, 1993), so it is a cross they have to bear in solitude.

In the clinic, a man is already reduced to the role of 'Man the sperm provider' (see Chapter 10), where his primary role (see also passage about Peter Humm in Chapter 7) is to be the sperm 'donor', apart from which he remains the helpless onlooker. To add insult to injury, he is not allowed to prove his manhood by producing the sample in the normal way, but he must do so by masturbation (see Chapter 8). Men do not use the word 'wanker' to describe an inadequate male without reason, thus to be reduced to being the onlooker, the 'provider' and the 'wanker' (to boot), places a man in a most humiliating position. To have to do all this when you are told that you have poor sperm is almost too much. In some cases, where even this limited role is taken away, for example in cases of azoospermia, it is too much altogether!

Thus, diagnosis of male infertility is the greatest blow that could happen to a man. As a consequence, as such couples progress through diagnosis and treatment, the man effectively enters a downward spiral. Men seem to have few resources with which to deal with the sentence of infertility. Often the only resource they have is their partner. Female ideology allows women to support each other, men's unfortunately does not.

Notes on counselling

Counselling is about dealing with client behaviour; their interaction with their environment at any given point in time. It is based on the idea that human development tends towards healthy growth. The helping relationship therefore consists of a partnership between client and counsellor working in collaboration to solve problems by activating client assets, skills and resources to help the client to deal with issues affecting his or her life (Egan, 1990; Rogers, 1951). In doing so the counsellor uses his or her own skills such as empathy (the ability to engage in human relations), active listening, ability to focus on expressed and unexpressed feelings, ability to feedback and reflect, to be able to offer clients respect and to appear genuine. Egan suggests that counselling relies on a working relationship and that the counsellor requires communication skills, the ability to help challenge the client's ideas or beliefs, ability to help clarify problems, to help set goals and implement them, to be able to carry out ongoing evaluation and to be able to help the client to develop skills themselves. The counsellor should be competent and adept at facilitation (helping the client to make their own decisions and to control their own actions). They must also be trustworthy and have a clear code of conduct and practice (British Association of Counselling or British Infertility Counselling Association have codes of practice which their counsellor members adhere to).

Rogers (1951) stressed the value of client-centred work. Here the client is the focus of the attention. The key to Rogers' teachings are that the client's right to autonomy is of utmost importance and that the counsellor is only there to facilitate the client's journey towards dealing with his or her issues, in such a way that he or she (the client) is in control and arrives at a solution through his or her own resources. Egan (1990) has described

Notes on counselling *continued*

a three-stage model which I have found most useful and very much in keeping with the client-centred theme. Briefly, Egan suggests that Stage 1 involves looking at the present scenario, which means that the client and counsellor go through a process of *identifying, exploring* and *clarifying*. Stage 2 is about looking at the preferred scenario, examining *goals* and *objectives*. Stage 3 involves getting there. The stages may be further broken down as follows:

Stage I
(a) story
(b) identify and challenge blind spots
(c) leverage (dealing with issues which might meaningfully make a difference)

Stage II
(a) look at range of future possibilities
(b) create viable agendas, choices and commitment

Stage III
(a) brainstorming, look at various strategies
(b) choose best strategies
(c) plan action

Each stage may overlap and interchange from one stage or sub-stage to another is common.

The meaning of fatherhood

At this point it is interesting to speculate on what fatherhood means to a man. Boys, like girls, grow up expecting to have all that others normally have. When things do not go according to plan, a major crisis has to be dealt with. A man's expectations in life, like women's, are likely to be influenced by the role models experienced during his childhood (Bee & Mitchell, 1984; Hite, 1991; Levinson, 1978). These role models may play a vital part in determining how men deal with infertility and by understanding this aspect, we may know how they might be better prepared to deal with such emotional issues. Even today, most families still consist of a unit headed by a father and a mother. Family life, though somewhat fragmented, still involves having children and in the main, most family pastimes centre on activities for the whole family unit, but generally concentrating on entertaining children (notice the spread of theme parks such as Thorpe Park and Alton Towers in the UK and Disney World and EuroDisney in the US and France). A strong experience is usually imbued in men therefore to follow the same role model provided by their father and their mother (Bee & Mitchell, 1984; Hite, 1991; Levinson, 1978). One common expectation from parents and peers is that a man will grow up, marry, have children and have grandchildren. Thus far, little is different from a woman's expectations. The desire to fulfil one's expectations is a powerful human necessity (Strathern, 1992). Thus to men, the idea of becoming a father means comradeship, a fulfilment of one's need to mimic our role models, being able to pass on a person's heritage and genes, being able to leave something behind (Mason, 1993). In terms of male ideology, having children also confirms a man's virility by providing visual confirmation for all to see. In the western world, becoming a man means the right to work, right to drive a car, and a right to be married and have children (Bee & Mitchell, 1984; Hite, 1991; Monach, 1993).

Male rites of passage in the past involved rituals of hunting (Mac-Cormack & Strathern (eds.), 1980). Man the hunter provided for his family. Young men would therefore be trained to hunt and to fight. Warfare was one of the great rituals of manhood. In the western world many of these rituals have been undermined and are to a great extent lost in time (see Chapter 1). In many ways manhood has lost much meaning in today's society. Hence the crisis that men now find themselves in and the importance of fatherhood, one of the last great icons of manhood. If the theme dealt with in Chapter 1 is accurate and man is rapidly having to adjust to a society which is becoming more favourable to female ideology, we must explore how men will cope and adjust themselves to a changing world, where many more women will be in employment, women will be more independent, women will be more eager to undergo divorce. One response is already beginning to emerge as a possible future role for men, that of suicide (Greenstein, 1993). As women are seizing the initiative, more and more men are now committing suicide (Samaritans' Press Release 1994). Are we expected too much from men in the home now? Michel Odent (1994) feels that too much is expected of men today in comparison to their traditional role in childbirth (that of the expectant father, waiting in the wings). Are we losing too many of our old rituals?

Summary of outlook and what needs to be done

Diagnosis is a fundamentally shattering event. Infertility diagnosis has often been compared with life crisis. Although men clearly enter into a crisis situation (Parry, 1990), when they are given their diagnosis of infertility (i.e. they experience loss, loss of control, humiliation and an uncertain future; their core belief and expectation of fatherhood is challenged; they become guilty, angry and depressed), men very rarely request crisis counselling. Over the years, I have done very little crisis work with men. I think this is because of the massive denial that seems to take over in most cases. Thus men attend counselling sessions mainly as a means of demonstrating support for their partners. In other words, their partners see the need for their men to undertake counselling, but because the men will not seek it themselves, a method of subterfuge is devised, where the female partner suggests that she would like to have some counselling (thereby assuming the blame and responsibility, which allows the male psyche to take part and potentially benefit from the process).

As mentioned in Chapter 4, for women, often the issues that arise which are listed below are likened to those of bereavement (although, bear in mind, this is not the only model).

- surprise
- denial
- anger
- isolation
- grief
- acceptance

(Mahlstedt, 1985; Menning 1980)

However, once again, perhaps because of the male's ability to deny issues, men rarely undertake the process of bereavement (a rare case is included in Case History 6.1 below), let alone bereavement counselling. Thus, where women are able to benefit from this specialist type of counselling, in my experience men rarely seek it (see also Mason, 1993).

The provision of counselling is vital therefore, if we are to avoid further isolating and abandoning these men. As the men begin to adjust to their diagnosis they need urgent attention, not just with regard to research, but also in terms of dealing with their actual emotional responses. Acceptance of being a genetic cul-de-sac takes time, support and understanding. We need to explore how best to deal with men's emotions and how best to provide them with facilitated access to both crisis and bereavement counselling.

With regard to DI, it seems that no man is able to fully embrace this option (see Chapter 9). It is also important to acknowledge that even modern treatment of male infertility centres on surgery for the fertile female partner. This lack of tangible treatment for the man himself leads to isolation, loss of self esteem and a feeling of uselessness (Lee, 1995a; Mason, 1993). We therefore need to urgently investigate the needs of men regarding their marginalisation. We also need to address the fact that men attend insufficiently to their own needs, being all too frequently ready to shoulder blame (Greenstein, 1993; Lee, 1995a; Mason, 1993). We must further explore the male experience of infertility. In terms of the science, it seems that progress in understanding male infertility will help by providing men, who have a strong need for information, in order to understand their physiological plight.

We must also remember that at whatever point counselling is taken up (on initial diagnosis, during treatment, when considering treatment options, during treatment or on cessation of treatment) the needs of the clients may vary enormously. For some it is a question of letting go and accepting the situation, in other words working through a process like bereavement. For others it is a matter of alleviating some of the worst feelings, anxieties, fears and worries. One must act bearing in mind that flexibility is useful and that men's response to infertility/subfertility may depend on the treatment options given/available to them. A model for counselling is outlined below.

Model for counselling infertile men

At this point, it might be useful to summarise my model for counselling when dealing with male infertility. It is by no means complete (nor ever will be), but to date, in its current dynamic state, it has been influenced by all the aforementioned observations. This is by no means a comprehensive text on 'how to counsel', but a simple demonstration of how the model might be used. Case history 6.1 contained within this description of the model 'counselling in action' is an amalgam of several different case histories, which has been done in order to provide as wide a range of experiences as possible for the reader in order to demonstrate the principles of the model.

Before each new session with a client or clients I introduce myself. I am sure it is not the ideal way of doing so, but its current state in evolution is as follows:

'Hello, how do you do, my name is Sammy Lee and I am a counsellor here at the ... clinic. I see counselling as an opportunity to deal with issues in a free and open manner, where the presence of a counsellor, who is trained to offer non-judgmental and objective input in a way family and close friends are often unable to, may be useful, particularly in a confidential and safe environment.

The counselling is client-centred; meaning that you (both) are held in high respect and you may be sure that there is no question of assessment. The sessions will be treated as confidential, though information may be shared with other members of the clinic team. The only circumstances where I might break confidentiality would possibly be in circumstances where your life or others might be at risk, particularly when considering the 'welfare of children', which is enshrined in law and is prescribed in the HFEA's code of practice.

A counselling session lasts for 50 minutes and I generally offer contracts of up to six sessions. If, at the end of this first session, you feel happy to confirm the contract, we will continue for a further five sessions during the next five weeks. If you are unhappy the contract may be terminated there and then. At the end of a contract, if further counselling is needed, I might consider the second contract, after which I would refer on if more counselling or specialist care was indicated (I am always happy to work closely with GPs, psychologists, psychotherapists or psychiatrists, where needed).'

Note that I do not see myself as offering long-term intervention, whereas a conventional counsellor may, but I believe short-term intervention has distinct advantages for many people and particularly men.

The counselling is a synthesis of client-centred work (non-judgmental and the client is given positive regard) and Egan's three-stage model (for a summary see *Notes on counselling* on page 74) and is obviously influenced greatly by Dr Sue Jennings, with whom I am proud to have worked and to have been associated. The direction of the sessions is dictated by the client, within the confines of certain boundaries in accordance with the structured way I carry out my initial exploration.

Exploration

The client must be engaged. This involves establishing a trusting and safe environment for the client. As I have mentioned earlier, women are usually tremendously supportive of their partners. Up to nine in ten clients will come to counselling with their female partner in attendance. This is often very useful in helping to establish initial contact with the client. Once an empathetic relationship has been established the exploration process may begin. The client's diagnosis, his feelings about it, his fears, his hopes, etc. (see above) will be explored. A major skill in this process centres on the use of metaphors. Even the most silent man will engage when he is allowed to use his own metaphors (in fact, once a man is engaged, he will even offer up some of his innermost feelings and emotions through the *gift* of his metaphors).

Almost always, I find we are dealing with angry and frustrated men who feel rather guilty and very much to blame. Loss of self esteem is likely, but will often be denied. There may be issues of punishment (see also Chapter 4) as well, but these will also tend to be in the background. Before beginning the exploration, I will make a quick assessment about the male client. There are many different types of male personalities, but in general I find the men often like to present themselves as the strong silent types.

Case history 6.1

Mr X is 39 years of old and is married to Mrs X who is 34 years old. After five years of infertility, they have recently been told that Mrs X has no obvious problems, insofar as she is ovulatory (has a 28–30 day cycle), has tubal patency and normal pelvic anatomy. During the past year, more of the focus within the infertility clinic has centred on Mr X who has just been told that, although his count and motility is normal, almost all his sperm (more than 95%) have an abnormal morphology. As a consequence of the diagnosis, a diagnostic IVF attempt has shown that at present, the sperm are unable to fertilise any of Mrs X's ova (ten were collected during the IVF attempt). In a state of shock at the IVF result, Mr and Mrs X are now considering their options and have asked to be referred for counselling.

I often begin the session by saying to Mr and Mrs X, 'I have been given some details by your clinic, but it may be useful for you to tell me your story (this allows me to begin to learn their language and, in the course of their story, I hope they will perhaps offer me some of their own valuable metaphors and possibly some images). If you agree, perhaps you might like to begin Mr X?'

Mr X leans back in his chair and folds his arms. He does not need much time to assess his thoughts. He slowly tells his story; he is very angry about the 'wasted years', as he put it, during which his wife was 'unnecessarily mucked about with'. At first, because the blame was 'naturally enough' put on his wife, he felt useless and helpless in all the clinic visits, so much so that he often did not go himself, leaving his wife to 'bear the brunt'; after all 'it was a gynaecology clinic, wasn't it?' Later on, when they finally suggested that he had 'male infertility', Mr X reports that he was 'gutted' (tears begin to well in his eyes, but they are forced back). At this point Mr X is now in full flow, the arms are unfolded and he is highly animated and leaning forward in earnest. Mrs X supports her husband's story by occasional interjections and nods of the head. Mr X goes on to say 'I feel like a wally now, really guilty ... all that time [she] carried the blame and in fact it was me; I am only really firing blanks!' At this point Mr X's story is finished for the time being. The time has come to reflect, summarise and feedback, using as much of Mr X's language as possible.

After a pause, I say '... this seems a good moment for me to summarise what you have said to me. You are clearly and understandably angry about the 'wasted years', and your wife being 'unnecessarily mucked about with'. You were also 'gutted' by the diagnosis of male infertility and clearly deeply upset by the failed IVF, which made you feel 'like a wally' and now you feel like you have only been 'really firing blanks!' Have I understood you properly? Mr X confirms the aptness of the summary.

Mr X was clearly devastated by the failure of his sperm to fertilise any of his partner's ova. He was depressed and was finding it hard to cope

Case history 6.1 *continued*

with work and life. He felt tired all the time and seemed plagued by the infertility, seemingly finding it hard to understand how and why he was in this position (of infertility).

When looking at his self esteem and his view of himself, he stated 'I feel like I have been broken . . . I feel useless, as if I am on the scrap heap.' I ask 'Is there no light at the end of the tunnel?' He shakes his head indicating no. He is infertile and will never have a child of his own, this is almost too much to bear. He feels he may never get over this.

Before winding up the first session we explore possible ways of bolstering his self esteem and marshalling some of his resources (look at possible support from family, parents, siblings and his partner). The first session is closed with an agreement to continue.

During the second and third sessions, we continue to explore issues surrounding Mr X's depression and anger. We explore whether there are issues relating to machismo; if he feels that his manhood is threatened by his infertility. There is no impotence and although he feels that men must not cry, and not seek help, the issues of silence, isolation and marginalisation are at the forefront regarding his pain and depression. He especially points out that part of the pain lies in the fact that he feels that 'the whole world knows and is laughing at me'.

During these two sessions I have to consider his depression and make a decision to refer if necessary (no referral is made). We also explore the topic of male ideology and try to examine how this might play a role in Mr X's feelings and responses to his plight. I begin to challenge some of Mr X's feelings relating to his isolation and hurt, pointing out that the way men behave in life ill equips them to deal with male infertility. Does he feel depressed because men like to be in control? Infertility takes this away, since potency is often linked to fertility; furthermore infertility clinics emasculate men, rendering them powerless and dependent. I ask him to consider the truth of this possibility and explore with him how he may adjust so that he might feel more positive about himself (this is an agreed goal for him at the end of the second session).

We also explore his own perception of his needs and I take care to watch for signs of crisis. We explore how individuals might cope under these circumstances and consider how he might cope or survive. We discuss various coping strategies such as a determination to undergo anything and everything or the opposite, to accept the condition of childlessness. We discuss how denial might detrimentally affect a person's decision-making capability and explore the issue of adulthood, adult expectations and the demands of parenthood. Mr X is surprised when I raise the issue of ambivalence in men; how some men are intimidated by real responsibility.

Insight and new understanding

Through the process of exploration and challenge insight may be achieved. Once insight has been established there is the possibility of 'moving on'. The model is non-directive and client-centred, thus when insight is achieved goal-setting becomes a possibility. The process of goal-setting is never imposed. Once again the use of metaphors and, where the client agrees, visualisation are invaluable in helping to move a client on towards new understanding.

Case history 6.1 (continued)

During the third session Mr X reports that he always feels 'hot'. Furthermore, there are days when he feels hot and confined in a 'blackness which seems to be all enveloping'. He is terrified of ending up as a childless bitter old man and fears the loneliness of this scenario. I ask Mr X 'are you able to tell me more about this hotness that you describe?' Mr X says that he finds it hard to define. I continue 'I may be barking up the wrong tree, but is it possible that at times you feel like you are locked in a dark furnace with no way out? Are you being punished?' Mr X agrees that it is one way of looking at it, but he is not quite sure whether he feels he is being punished or not, but the feelings of hotness and the enveloping darkness are quite oppressive. I ask 'is there no way out of this hot dark place?' Mr X ponders for a while and replies that he is not sure. I suggest the following: 'wherever and whatever it is made of, is there no light anywhere or is it not possible that we might be able to find a door which might lead to a way out?' Mr X is not wholly enthusiastic about it, but he is willing at least to consider the possibility that a way out might be possible.

It occurs to me that Mr X might benefit from some bereavement work. Working with his metaphors, we tried some work to look at his loss. We worked with his fantasies. He was willing to conjure up his 'dream child' (Jennings, 1995) and talked of how he would have wanted to take the child to football matches (boy or girl) or to the park or zoo (as Jennings has pointed out, grieving for a child that never actually existed is very hard. By visualising the fantasy child, it seems to help make the child 'real', thereby facilitating the process of bereavement which, Jennings has reported, can be a very long process when dealing with infertility in both men and women).

Action and goal setting

We explore the range of possibilities and the client decides which goal he and his partner will aim for. By examining the issues, confronting one's emotions and dealing with them through action, clients will be better placed to impose their own will on the direction of their lives. In this setting, one of the most important issues is that they be able to make well informed decisions on their treatment.

The use of visualisation has also been a vital tool. When a man is in despair, he may often be brought out of it by asking him to visualise his feelings. Having attached the emotions to a 'real' object, 'a light at the end of the tunnel' may materialise.

Case history 6.1 (continued)

With respect to Mr X's picture of himself, we used the visualisation process to explore how he viewed himself. Here we did a little bit of art work. Mr X drew a picture of himself (similar to the picture in Fig. 4.1), except that the image of the man was covered in cracks. Mr X felt that he was breaking apart. Here Mr X could see some 'light at the end of the tunnel'. Initially we looked at how he might be held together with some tape. Later, the tape was replaced by a lacquer, until eventually the cracks disappeared, but the man still could not smile. Perhaps this might be dealt with at some future point.

Back to new insight

Egan (1990) states that counselling does not always progress in the stages as described and that often after goals have been set, we may return to further exploration, challenging or to new insight yet again and so on and so forth. We do not always pass each stage in sequential order and it might be appropriate, at times to bypass a stage and to return later. Thus when Mr X attends for the fourth session, his news and position is not surprising:

Case history 6.1 (continued)

Mrs X starts the session by reporting a surprising change in Mr X. He has been less depressed recently. Mr X reports that he has had time to reflect and that he now feels that he does feel that he is being punished and even punishing himself. The infertility is his burden for being a bad person. He has felt less hot of late and the enveloping blackness does not seem so oppressive now.

We seem to be making progress, so I look to moving Mr and Mrs X on, 'how might we now see the future?' The question surprises Mr and Mrs X. Mrs X asks about DI as an option, we explore the importance for them of biological and social parenthood. We discuss in earnest the issue of men who cannot give up hope regarding treatment. I now further challenge their perception of their situation, in an attempt to invoke realism and to

---

Case history 6.1 *continued*

move them on so that they will be able to cope with day to day life and to be empowered to make decisions about their future.

Unfortunately, time is limited and I remind them there are now only two sessions left. Mr and Mrs X agree to the goal of spending some time together to consider their options seriously. I am aware that Mrs X looks as if she has much to say about herself, yet these are essentially Mr X's sessions and I must give him priority. I make a mental note to offer Mrs X referral if she wishes it.

Surprisingly, Mrs X does not attend the fifth session. Mr X makes an excuse for Mrs X, but it quickly becomes clear, there is a disagreement about how they will face the future. Mrs X, it seems wishes to have DI, but Mr X is not so sure. We therefore further explore and challenge Mr X's expectations. His expectancy of fatherhood, how male ideology itself reinforces men's helplessness in the infertility clinics, an exploration of his own role models and his childhood are all considered. Mr X discloses that he feels the lack of biological fatherhood stops him from achieving fulfilment and joining the ranks of 'real' men. He states he is not ambivalent and would welcome the opportunity of assuming real responsibility. However, and there are tears in his eyes when he reveals this, he has considered the option of DI long and hard, but cannot yet accept DI as an option and is willing to face childlessness. The remainder of the session is taken up by exploring ways he may communicate to Mrs X his true feelings. I challenge his belief that he has made all his feelings clear to Mrs X. I suggest that maybe he has been too manly when talking to Mrs X and not shown the depth of his true feelings. The session is closed by an agreement that Mr X will take action and allow Mrs X to see that he has deep emotions about the issue of DI and is not unwilling purely from the point of being unhelpful and obstructive.

For the sixth session I am pleased to see both Mr and Mrs X attend. I remind them that this is the last session. We look at the future and weigh up the options; DI or not DI. Mr X feels that he is much clearer in his mind now about his future. Mr and Mrs X will continue to discuss the pros and cons of DI together. Nevertheless, Mr X points out that if they decide not to proceed with further treatment, he now feels able to look forward. He acknowledges the value of having undergone a bereavement type exercise after an earlier session when bereavement had been explored. He discloses that he has now symbolically laid to rest his fantasy children and accepted that he might now never take his son to a football match or his son and daughter to the zoo with Mrs X.

Mrs X reports that life at home is much more on an even keel now; the shock of IVF failure had brought a great deal of tension to the home, which was now dispelled. They still have many hurdles and trials and tribulations to undergo, but they now feel they can face them with a more optimistic outlook. I point out that Mr X has had the lion's share of the time in our sessions and ask Mrs X if she feels there are any issues she

> **Case history 6.1** *continued*
>
> might like to disclose at this late stage. She becomes tearful and states that she still desperately wants a child, but she notes her husband's pain and feelings regarding DI. Mr X reaches for her hand and they cry together. I invite Mrs X to ask for referral if she feels the need (I wonder if I should be directive, but decide against it); Mrs X shakes her head indicating no.
>
> I feel that we have left so much unsaid and done so little, but nevertheless, I offer a resumé of where we began, where we travelled and where we have ended up. In the closing statement of my summary I say 'a key issue for the immediate future now appears to be whether to have DI or not'. I try to offer a parting goal saying 'do you both think it would be useful and possible to keep talking openly and honestly about your feelings on the matter of DI?' They both assent. I offer again a referral to another counsellor who I suggest may be able to throw new light on the matter as well as attending more to Mrs X's needs. They also agree to this. I close the session and wish them well for the future.
>
> It is hard to know how this case will end, but if they choose DI, they will need further counselling regarding the implications of treatment.

To summarise, the model is based on Egan's three-stage model (exploration–new insight–action), with the power of metaphors and visualisation as additional vital ingredients. As we begin to understand more, and with greater personal experience of counselling, the model is bound to evolve.

Conclusion

Much of the information discussed in this chapter makes it reasonable to speculate that male ideology is assimilated throughout early childhood. It is reinforced on a daily basis with the subconscious collusion of females (mother and sisters), because the system has become powerfully insidious and all pervasive (Crawshaw, 1995; Hite, 1991). By teenage and adulthood, male ideology is so powerfully established that it dominates all aspects of Western life (Hite, 1991; Greenstein, 1993; Ortner, 1974). The paradox is that men have become so steeped in the lore of their supremacy, that male ideology 'chops their legs off at the knees', when they are given a diagnosis of male infertility (Lee, unpublished observation). The blow to their belief system is so severe that many go into total denial in order to survive. The men are unequipped to deal with the fact that their expectations of fatherhood are under severe threat. Because men do not cry and men cope, they become isolated and effectively marginalised by the system, which again paradoxically colludes against them (Lee, 1995a; Lee, unpublished observation).

Since male ideology is so pervasive, most people, male and female are also ill-equipped to deal with men who have been challenged by male infertility. This in itself leads to a conspiracy of silence, where no-one is able to acknowledge the reality of the situation, so historically (and in many clinics still) the focus shifts and remains on the woman, who must bear the burden. Even worse for the female partner, she must usually endure and support the male, (1) because she has always been trained to do this and (2) compassionately, she is probably the man's only real means of resource (Lee, unpublished observation; Mason, 1993). Feminist ideology, though helping to redress the balance, is in itself not helpful in the long term. Men will be helped best by allowing themselves access to their creative personality and by adopting many of the positive aspects of female (non-feminist) ideology (Lee, unpublished observation; Van Hoose & Worth, 1982).

As mankind continues to mature and develop, this difficult phase that man is going through (man in crisis) should end in a positive transformation, much in the way that a butterfly emerges from the chrysalis. Until then, we need to understand all the above and learn ways to support men without threatening their belief system and thereby their very existence.

A public acknowledgement of the existence of male infertility and the ignorance surrounding it may lead to more openness about it and therefore less public stigma about male infertility. Perhaps more access to counselling will also help to alleviate the stigma, anxieties and the *isolation*. We need to further explore the intensity and pain of diagnosis and for the need and nature of *support*; is it useful to know that they are not alone? Is it useful speaking with others in the same plight? How much time is needed to adjust, to cope with male infertility? We need to explore a man's need to be a father; how men view fatherhood. Finally and by no means the least we need to explore the role of stress and how its reduction will help.

If we are able to attend to some of the research outlined above we should be able to provide effective access to counselling for men. We will be able to provide better support and therapeutic intervention for them. It is to be hoped that the social stigma of male infertility will continue to be eroded and that ultimately, we will be able to overcome the isolation that accompanies a diagnosis of male infertility.

Chapter 7
Crucial Differences in Male and Female Ideology and the Role of Childhood Development

Introduction

I do not intend to get into any controversial discussions here over whether the ideas of Freud, Piaget, Eysenck *et al.* have more merit or not. This is certainly not my brief nor would it serve any useful purpose. The reason for considering childhood development of men and women is to see if we might throw some light on why men behave as they do. Some ground has already been covered in previous chapters, nevertheless, the topic deserves an extensive review in a chapter of its own. Why then do men behave as they do? Are their responses truly different from women's? Can childhood development explain this?

Male ideology and theories on how it is perpetuated

Shere Hite (1991) suggests that male ideology (for a definition see the Introduction) is built up on a historically based culture system rather than a biological one. 'Men being, women giving' is her simplistic view of things. She suggests that psychological stereotyping has given men an advantage. Men therefore get preferential treatment and superior social status. This system fills the tiniest cracks in the minds of both men and women and it is, as a result, self-repeating and all pervasive. A detailed description of Hite's definition of male ideology has been given in the introduction to this book.

Ortner (1974) and others (Crawshaw, 1995; MacCormack, 1980a; Monach, 1993) have discussed gender-based differences in male ideology and whilst not every culture or society follows the above-mentioned features (see MacCormack & Strathern (eds.), 1980), most men in Western society are exposed to the type of ideology that Hite describes (consider that New Man, who sees woman as his equal, remains a myth, as discussed in the main introduction).

Just like women, men also need support, but unlike women, men do not seek support from their peers (Lee, 1995a; Mason, 1993). In the home, however, they need and demand support from their partners for their emotional requirements, thereby placing enormous demands on their spouses (this is especially true in the arena of male infertility). This in turn may partly explain how children perceive and then reinforce their concentration on the male role player (Hite, 1991). The female spouse gives the male the attention he craves and needs; the children observe this role being played out, introject it and thus the stereotype is reinforced in both male and female children (Hite, 1991). The female child learns to be like Mum and to pander to the male, whilst the male child learns to expect to be superior to his female peers. 'Don't disturb Daddy, he is tired from work' is a common theme, and because of the stereotyping no-one thinks to ask 'what about Mum?'

Women who perpetuate male ideology play a role which is feminine to their children, which means they must be dutiful, be polite, be passive, not argue, not be tough, put other people before themselves (the Bible says this too, but this should not be surprising since the Bible also perpetrates and perpetuates these sex roles, whether by wilful male mistranslation or otherwise). In general these women tend to put the family first and themselves in a distant last place. At this point, we might ask the following question: are male attributes such as aggression, competitiveness, being strong, etc., the norm or the result of social brainwashing? When considering this question, we can look at a number of scenarios before answering it. Marriage is a sharing relationship which is based on reciprocal emotions. We might suppose that support should be given equally if it is meant to be a true partnership. However, this is not necessarily so in all marriages. Even in infertility clinics, we can see that marriage in this setting is unequal, since IVF is all about women. Men show their partners support by being stereotypical man; stoic, strong, silent, paying for the treatment. They rarely show real emotional support for their spouses (Lee, unpublished observation; Mason, 1993). Rather they demand support from their spouses (as their mothers nurtured them so that they were able to adapt to male ideology, so must their partners play a similar role). So much so that when it comes to male infertility clinics, 90% of the time the female supports the spouse by attending the consultation and often being the person volunteering all the information and often taking the lead, whilst men often leave their partners on their own in fertility or gynaecology clinics (Lee, 1995a).

Women's response to male ideology

Hite (1991) suggests that traditionally men withhold equal companionship. They distance themselves emotionally. They always have the sanction of violence which women rarely have. Women and men's culture are in fact two worlds with some interlocking sets of values (see MacCormack, 1980 for an overview). Women want to share and love. Men want to be valued for their work role. In order to redress the balance, in my opinion, women are no longer willing to settle for the fair-value system but are adopting male ideology, which threatens the male world (Greenstein, 1993). This has resulted in a cultural conflict, which has been discussed extensively in Chapter 1. Men's greatest weakness is this emotional isolation which paradoxically enhances their need to be loved (while not being able to show true reciprocation?). There is therefore great ambiguity. Real closeness is threatening to a man. 'Real men' never completely let down their guard, or lose control. Real men must always assert control, assert their independence. Real closeness makes men vulnerable.

Sex roles and child development

Herein perhaps, lies the answer to the question posed earlier. This male ideology is deeply ingrained in society (Hite, 1991). It is a strong stereotype. It has become the norm through brainwashing (over centuries). Whichever theory we accept for the childhood development of different sex-role models, most hypotheses make the assumption that sex-role behaviour is learnt. Throughout life, the child is presented with models which it may imitate. In most cases, the child gradually identifies with its own sex (rightly or wrongly) thereby adopting certain kinds of behaviour. The 'right kind' of behaviour may be reinforced, perhaps generally by the approving parent(s), or perhaps through Freud's theory or even that of status envy. Eventually (by whatever mechanism) most children then learn to behave in the way considered appropriate for its sex (this is known as operant conditioning–imitation and identification).

Margaret Mead (1996) did research which may be taken as providing evidence that sex roles are learned, in her cross-cultural studies. In particular, among the Tchambuli tribe of New Guinea, the sex roles are reversed. The women do the work, make the decisions and control the household, while the men take on the role of being not very sensible, being the more artistic, fretful, irresponsible, wearers of jewellery, gossipers and quarrelers. Women are considered strong, capable and serious – quite the opposite of recent western sex roles. As in the West, these differences are expected in the children. By the age of 10 or 11, the girls are very different from the boys. They are already more alert and enterprising, whilst the boys are timid and generally unable to concentrate on things. Other work (Gillison, 1980; Goodale, 1980; Jennings, 1995; Strathern, 1980) shows that not all cultures necessarily follow the Western patterns and that indeed, other societies have different ways of allowing women access to decision making in society.

In our own world, children learn their sex roles in many different ways, through their parents, from television, through the different toys that are marketed (for example, for boys – uniforms, military equipment, boys wear blue; for girls – dolls, fashion, nursing outfits, girls wear pink) and through children's books or comics and so on and so forth. According to Adcock (1976) we must allow for the different toys that male and female children are given (as above) as well as bearing in mind that boys tend to leave school earlier. Physiologically girls develop faster than boys and women excel verbally, whereas boys excel spatially. Adcock reports that girls are more cooperative than boys. British public schools may also have contributed greatly to male role models. Here the stiff upper lip is a glorious stereotype, one of the factors by which it is claimed that the British Empire was won.

At the end of the day, it seems clear that the male ideology that Hite describes is not based on genetics. Maccoby & Jacklin (1974) have shown that gender-based differences are in fact, largely based on myth rather than reality, but, as Masters and Johnson (Masters, Johnson & Kolodny, 1982) also point out, adult males and females display different behaviour, particularly around issues of fertility (Crawshaw, 1995; Monach, 1995; Scutt, 1990). They suggest that their own and modern research (Bee & Mitchell, 1984; MacCormack & Strathern (eds.), 1980; Maccoby & Jacklin, 1974; Van Hoose & Worth, 1982) in addition to Mead's now dated work show that gender-based behaviour is environmentally adapted rather than being based on genetics or in the mind.

Male and the new female ideologies in conflict

Concentration on performance, doing manly things, being manly, not crying. Men do (are active) and men do not rely. Women rely on men. These are the traditional roles (Hite, 1991). However, feminism and the gradual independence of woman has eroded the stranglehold that the above male ideology has maintained over the centuries (Greenstein, 1993). Women are now exercising much more freedom of choice. They are now able to choose to have longer careers, and if they decide to have children, there are more options available to them, whereby they may return to work within a few months of giving birth. If women deliberately choose their careers ahead of their motherhood role, reproduction technology has now given them the option of changing their minds. Women past the menopause may now still have children. Divorce has also empowered women. Many women may now open new chapters to their lives and escape from partners to whom they no longer wish to be tied. The public acceptance of single mothers is also evidence of a change in society. Men's role models have not yet adapted to this world where women's main role is no longer just motherhood. There exists a refractory delay.

We may further generalise that there is possibly more delinquency in males from school age onwards and that perhaps girls manifest nervous habits more. Males may be overtly more aggressive. How much of all this is actually dependent on sex roles remains unclear, but we may speculate. Men apply different rules in their interactions with other men and women (McCormack & Strathern (eds.), 1980). Western women have the ideology of love and nurture (Hite, 1991; MacCormack & Strathern (eds.), 1980). To give women equality is a challenge to male ideology (Greenstein, 1993). Male ideology states that someone must dominate and that person is the male. Female equality is a direct challenge on the male psyche. Bloch & Bloch (1980) have shown that traditionally, men are supposed to derive their dominance from their association with culture, which is seen as being handed down from God and that female intellect has been denounced, on the basis that women are associated with nature (which is often seen as being inferior to culture). Thus, because women are more natural, eighteenth century French and European thinking inferred that they were therefore predisposed to flights of fancy and loose thinking, and so unsuitable for serious manly pursuits such as politics.

Furthermore, Bloch & Bloch (1980) also suggest that men have a sort of subconscious fear of women, because they had a natural hold over them, and that women were dangerous because of their uncontrollable and disruptive nature as well as their polluting ability (presumably menstruation and childbirth). Issues concerning female power and pollution are further considered in Chapter 8. Throughout MacCormack & Strathern (eds.) (1980) there are allusions towards ancient female power and dominance (Greenstein, 1993) and in particular Gillison (1980) describes how the Gimi people of Papua New Guinea have myths (regarding possession of symbolic flutes) which refer to women's loss of power in the depths of prehistory.

Entering into a stable relationship with a woman is also a challenge to male ideology, since there is an implied reduction in independence and freedom. How can a 'real man' such as Rambo, a tough strong independent type, be tied down in a stable relationship? For some men entering into a relationship leads to great emotional struggle. In return for their position of dominance, men pay the cost of loneliness and isolation, and a constant feeling of conflict, since men cannot admit weakness (Lee, 1995a). Men must hold back their emotions, must always act rationally, and cannot talk to anyone about their problems or feelings.

As women begin to change value systems, men must begin to change as well. Dealing with male infertility often involves exploring men's values and producing movement in the way these men see things. Often, for those who are unable to see new possibilities, it is perhaps these who are most likely to have their marriage break down as a consequence of the infertility. When confronted with issues, men tend to withdraw. They face infertility in much the same way they face fights or arguments with their spouses. They try to maintain privacy. They are prepared to exit readily. If they stand and fight they fight dirty. The male club has rigid rules of behaviour and there are certain strict rituals.

Indeed, male ideology is currently all pervasive, forming the basic building block of many religions whether they be Eastern, Western, Islamic, Christian, etc. Historically, only a few men have taught a more feminine ideology such as Jesus Christ who suggested turning the other cheek and Mahatma Gandhi who suggested passive resistance, a quite different strategy from the teachings of the wrathful and vengeful God of the Old Testament.

Hite (1991) suggests that as males undergo transition from boy to manhood, they are expected to drop all feminine mores. In doing so there is a type of severance from the mother which may fill some men with enormous guilt, hence the need to be a real mean hombre in order to compensate for the guilt. This guilt may also be important for some men when dealing with male infertility. This guilt may certainly be related to the theme of 'guilt and punishment' (Lee, unpublished observation) and may also possibly contribute to ambivalence in men.

A modern male's outlook on infertility

I shall conclude this chapter by looking at one man's personal description of his experience. Peter Humm (1989) offered a man's point of view of infertility treatment. Note that it is not male infertility in this case, hence he is more easily able to talk about his own experience. It would be much harder for a man with male infertility! His partner has also written about her experience. This couple give unique insight into a couple's viewpoint on infertility and its treatment. His abiding memory is one of waiting, always waiting. All this whilst Maggie, his wife, was examined, injected, tested, monitored and advised. He reports that even as he writes he still feels somewhat left out (as Maggie writes at the same time). He states that he must leave it to Maggie to describe what the men in white coats did, since he was left with a fraught gap, which only his imagination could fill. It is important to note that even though he did not have male infertility, he still felt very marginalised. He also comments on how he would never know how it felt to be treated since everything centred on his partner. Peter found it difficult, even after success, to let go of his experiences. He states that it is hard to know even now what all the years of waiting did to them as a couple. I am in no doubt that the seeking of medical help itself produces an iatrogenic process which may cause great harm to couples' relationships. In its extreme form, some couples will eventually seek separation and divorce.

Peter Humm reports that he always expected to have children. He describes feeling shock when fatherhood did not materialise. He then realised that 'what had seemed natural was only going to be achieved with deliberate effort and the dismaying involvement of intervention of many others'. He reports that instead of bringing them together, having a child was going to bring episodes of separation (travel for treatment) and that what should have been natural was going to be surrounded by technical language and alien procedures (medical intervention). Even though there was no evidence of male factor, he still reports episodes of doubt and actively having to avoid insecurity. He states that his masculinity was also tested by having to be the provider of sperm according to order. In his own words, the man in normal circumstances is 'reduced even more swiftly than usual to the momentary provider of sperm' (how bad a man must feel when he has infertility himself). Peter felt that he 'was removed to a distressing distance' away from all clinical matters; a matter of some distress to him.

Like many, not just in cases of male infertility, Peter reports that his sex life was greatly affected with the quickest pragmatic sex becoming the norm. He reports that infertility is like a merrygoround of changing states, such as the state of parenthood, the state of infertility, the state of wanting children and the state of accepted childlessness. These are all swings which desperately relied or centred on ongoing treatment or not. He states that medicine tends to separate the mind from the body and that the clinicians failed them by almost entirely *ignoring their psychological state*. He complains of medical condescension and their unrelenting insensitivity. Especially in this field, practitioners need reminding that their visions of the brave new world should be grounded in the real suffering and pain of their patients.

Peter coins a phrase: *coming out of the waiting room*. He feels that male infertility must do this. He makes some further salient points. He feels that there is a need for more female gynaecologists, that while we wait for this, the current male gynaecologists need to be more appreciative of their position and their treatment of their female patients. He suggests that the male partners of women under the care of gynaecologists need to stop colluding with the medics (a male conspiracy of silence) and that the husbands need to be more assertive when dealing with the medical profession. He says 'If I had been there during the tests and consultations, then Maggie might have been recognised as more than a test site for pioneering and risky therapies and I might have been seen more than – on every 9th and 14th day – the provider of sperm.'

Paradoxically, whilst the clinicians display their power and the power of medical patriarchy, the male partner of an infertility patient is marginalised, an unnatural place for a man. Yet these men end up here because they still want to play the role of protective men. The fear of losing one's position as husband paradoxically puts the man in an even deeper position of helplessness (in reality, Peter wishes he had been able in himself to get closer to the events in the clinic). Peter's epitaph for the whole episode when talking about photographs of their baby was as follows 'We did not send any to the consultant at the teaching hospital or to the relays of junior doctors whose treatment had ended in success.

We had not heard from them throughout the pregnancy. They remained in a separate world from ours.

Conclusion

Much of the information discussed in this chapter makes it reasonable to speculate that male ideology is assimilated throughout early childhood. It is reinforced on a daily basis with the subconscious collusion of females (mother and sisters), because the system has become powerfully insidious and all pervasive. By teenage and adulthood, male ideology is so powerfully established that it dominates all aspects of Western life. The paradox is that men have become so steeped in the lore of their supremacy, that male ideology chops their legs off at the knees, when they are given a diagnosis of male infertility. The blow to their belief system is so severe that many go into total denial in order to survive. The men are unequipped to deal with the fact that their expectations of fatherhood are under severe threat. Because men do not cry and men cope, they become isolated and effectively marginalised by the system, which again paradoxically colludes against them. Since male ideology is so pervasive, most people, male and female are also unequipped to deal with men who have been challenged by male infertility. This in itself leads to a conspiracy of silence, where noone is able to acknowledge the reality of the situation, so historically (and in many clinics still) the focus shifts and remains on the woman, who must bear the burden.

Even worse, for the female partner, she must usually endure and support the male, one – because she has always been trained to do this and two – compassionately, she is probably the man's only real means of resource. Feminist ideology though helping to redress the balance is in itself not helpful in the long term. Men will be helped best by allowing themselves access to their creative personality and in adopting many of the positive aspects of female (non-feminist) ideology. As mankind continues to mature and develop, this difficult phase that man is going through (man in crisis) should end in a positive transformation, much in the way that a butterfly emerges from the chrysalis. Until then, we need to understand all the above and learn ways to support men without threatening their belief system and thereby their very existence.

Chapter 8
A New Messianic Age and the Cults of Children and Fertility: Cultural, Ethnic and Religious Factors

Introduction

In multiracial societies, such as exist in the UK, the USA, Europe and Oceania, it is important to consider how the cultural, ethnic and religious background of our patients and clients may affect their outlook. Religion, in particular, plays a strong role in those who have strong beliefs and faith in their clergy and God. Through my own work with male infertility, I can confirm that culture, ethnic background and religion play a large role in the way people think and respond to infertility (Lee, 1995a).

People from non-Western backgrounds have an experience of medical models very different from ones we are used to in the West. Shamanism, fortune telling, healing and herbalism are all common forms of medicine, which here in the West are considered fringe. Nevertheless, for those whose ethnic backgrounds embrace these types of interventions, the acceptance of these as complementary treatments; in conjunction with our Western treatments, will almost certainly help to reduce the level of worry and anxiety that such patients might normally harbour. The impact of religion on infertility should not be underestimated. As I have alluded in Chapter 1, about man in crisis, whether people are overtly religious or not, religion pervades most Western societies, especially here in the UK, in Europe and in the USA. The notion of guilt and punishment may therefore be found not only in the roots of the Bible itself, but running through the veins of Western (European) history itself, so that in almost every culture of the West, the foundations of our beliefs and societies is based on religion.

A new Messianic age

Throughout the world, many societies have Messianic prophecies. Jews are still waiting for their Messiah of Davidic origins. Christians await Jesus Christ's second coming. The Aztecs thought that Don Hernando Cortés was their Messiah, at last arriving to save them as prophesied. In Britain, King Arthur and Excalibur, his sword, are slumbering, and will one day return, when Britain is in dire need of them. In times of crisis, people from all backgrounds look for a Messiah to appear and save them.

Keeping with the theme of man in crisis, it is noticeable that apocalyptic cults such as David Koresh's Branch Davidian (he perished along with many of his followers at Waco in the USA in 1993), or Aum in Japan, are becoming increasingly popular in Western societies and there is a continuing growth in the development of new cults. Our current crisis is not an original concept. Indeed history is littered with precedents. History has a way of repeating itself. Throughout time, and often at millennial landmarks, such as the timing of our present 'crisis', men and women have looked for the appearance of a Messiah. There seems to be a strong need in mankind for such symbols. Indeed, throughout the Bible mankind has always been looking for and has received a number of Messianic visitations.

For the many reasons already presented in Chapter 1, man (and woman) has reached the point of crisis; small wonder that in the USA, television evangelism has become so powerful. Television is a powerful medium. People today are highly susceptible to charismatic persons who are able to tap into the psyche of a mass conscience. This is because, in the West, the erosion of our roles and rituals (see Chapter 1) has left many people feeling that their lives are in disarray; the loss of defined boundaries in our roles and the disappearance of many rituals means that many of the things which used to be taken for granted (i.e. which used to be immutable) are no longer so, which means less continuity and more change (Strathern, 1992). Man has been here before, seen it, done it, and got the T-shirt! Throughout history people have lost their sense of direction and had to adjust to changing life. In the first century AD there was Jesus Christ in the Middle East, in the eighth century, Charlemagne and Roland in France, and later the Revolution in France in the eighteenth century, as well as the industrial revolution in Britain and most recently Hitler (the Antichrist) in Germany in this century. In other words, in times of need people search for a Messiah or something that will deliver them from their troubles and strife. Someone or something that will come to lead them out of trouble.

Life cycles, rebirth and the cult of children

It is interesting to note that the notion of a Messiah usually involves the idea of resurrection (Osiris, god of one of mankind's oldest recorded religions, is resurrected from death and now rules the underworld where all the dead will be judged. Jesus Christ is resurrected from death and sits at God's right hand where after Armageddon, the whole of mankind will also be subjected to Judgement Day). Symbolically the idea of rebirth is one of mankind's strongest myths (resurrection and rebirth may be equated with salvation). In many, if not most religions (except notably Buddhism), rebirth, being born into an afterlife on transition through death is seen as an ultimate reward for faith and adherence to teachings.

Goodale (1980) has found that the Kaulong people of New Britain believe that an adult who has no children loses his or her identity and may well be expected to commit suicide as a consequence of this lack of fertility. Marriage in their society is all about providing replacements for themselves (just as the Church sees it; procreation in the sanctity of marriage is all important). Thus, if the birth of a child has similar connotations for modern Western men, for instance, if we are in some way reborn through our children (leaving something behind, or being able to pass on our heritage; Mason, 1993), then children take on a new significance.

In Chapter 4, we looked at how some men (and women) may harbour a subconscious guilt, which might lead to feelings of unworthiness (being beyond redemption, thus with no chance of rebirth). This guilt may also ultimately have a physical manifestation, producing actual infertility, as a consequence of their feeling of 'badness' (i.e. this is their punishment). As I have mentioned in Chapter 1, a senior nursing officer once pointed out to me that in a large number of couples that we were treating (50% at the time), the female partner was by profession a teacher. Furthermore, in my work with male infertility, every male psychotherapist who has attended my clinic has had a peculiar form of severe oligozoospermia of unexplained origin. These two phenomena have further led me to wonder whether it is possible that persons working as teachers (female) or psychotherapists (male) are in some way able to suppress their own fertility, through the mechanism of guilt and punishment. Current thinking in infertility clinics is that psychologically rooted infertility does not exist. This is mainly because of the medical fraternity's need to 'pathologise' patients, which has led to the idea that some psychoanalysts in the 1970s introduced as the rather unfortunate speculation that there might exist an 'infertile personality' (see section on psychogenic infertility in Chapter 5).

If rebirth is symbolically linked with the idea of reproduction, it is worth considering that with the passage of time, through the millennia, we have moved away from the cyclical nature of life where history is not very important, since no events in time are unique and natural events repeat themselves, history therefore carries no great significance. The cyclical nature of life has dominated many traditions throughout the world. Many cultures still adhere to the idea of cyclicity (MacCormack & Strathern (eds.), 1980), but here in the Western world this is no longer true.

In modern times, however, we now have a linear model of time. History, therefore becomes more important and life must then adopt an importance in terms of its meaning. In the linear model, not only does history become more important, but man's religious expectations also change; the idea of Messianic salvation becomes much more important. In the linear model you only get one chance (in the cyclical model you are constantly reborn with limitless chances, where the ultimate aim is 'enlightenment', a very different philosophical background).

Bearing in mind the limitations of the linear model, if we see life after death (rebirth) as being a reward for faith, one aspect of salvation may be manifested in the symbolic and real nature of having a child. Continuing with this theme, it seems pertinent to wonder if becoming a parent has become the modern equivalent of a pilgrimage? As our symbols, rituals, old beliefs have all been eroded, are we now left with the *cult of children* as the last meaningful symbol in life? In the old religions there were always ceremonies involving ritual purification. The idea of sacred rebirthing is an important aspect of baptism (the Bible is full of incidents where people or mankind has been saved from water). Have these symbols been replaced because of the decline in traditional faiths?

With regard to the idea that we now have a cult of children, let us consider recent press and public interest (bordering on frenzy) over the tragic kidnapping and killing of young children (e.g. James Bulger), or the recent spate of abducted babies from hospital wards. All these events were headline front page news items, relegating important world events to the inner pages. Witness too the resistance during the recent great depression of the 1980s and early 1990s. Despite continuing recession and record levels of home repossessions, families still managed to spend record amounts on children's video games and computers. It seems that children fill a more central role in our lives than ever before.

The cult of fertility

Somehow, the issue of fertility has been caught up in this crisis. Certainly as discussed in the main introduction and in Chapters, 1, 4, 5 and 6, a diagnosis of infertility may lead to crisis in some individuals. Furthermore, one possible manifestation of a person in general crisis might be a reduction in his or her fertility. What seems clear is that if we have a cult of children, then fertility itself must assume a new importance. Thus we equally have a new fertility cult, a modern day version of something that has existed since the dawn of mankind.

In many ancient religions the female is the more important sex. She always represents fertility. Isis, one of the early fertility goddesses belonged to the Egyptians and her Sumerian counterpart is Inanna. Both goddesses were responsible for bringing the fertile part of the season to the year. In Sumerian myth, Inanna spends some time away from the Earth; visiting the underworld to search for her dead sister. This story was probably used as a means of explaining a period of famine. In the same way, Isis was responsible for the annual flooding of the Nile which brought fertility to the delta and the banks running alongside the river from the fifth cataract down to the delta itself. It was Isis who played a key role in the rebirth (resurrection) of her husband Osiris, who had been killed by his jealous brother Set. Osiris had been dismembered and his remains scattered throughout the world. Isis recovered all her husband's parts save the phallus, but was able to resurrect him and, equally importantly, able to conceive through the reborn Osiris, a son called Horus. Hence we can see the doubly important idea of resurrection and rebirth in one of the oldest myths known to man (and the star role was played by a woman of power and resource).

Fertility is a universal human concern (Fig. 8.1). In every society in this world irrespective of culture, beliefs, religion, infertility brings great anguish. Almost every society has rituals and prayers related to successful conception and confinement. Equally so, when things go wrong, many cultures have their own way of explaining why things have gone wrong. For example, in some cultures, blame will be laid at the door of the individual who must have upset the gods or a neighbour in some

The Reproduction Revolution
Lecture by Dr S. Lee

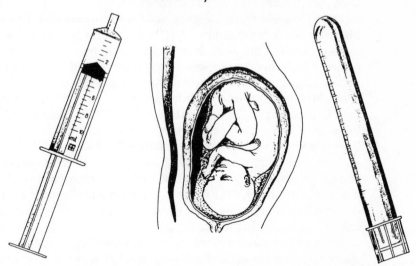

Figure 8.1 *The reproduction revolution.* It brings great advance and offers humanity many options, not all good. It also brings reproduction without sex, which is paradoxical, since Carl Djerassi gave us sex without reproduction in the 1960s whilst Steptoe and Edwards gave us reproduction without sex in the 1980s. The reproduction revolution is still gathering pace. So much so that the public imagination has been well and truly caught; to such an extent that their appetite knows no bounds. Public lectures on the revolution are always well attended.

way, thus bringing about ill fortune. They may blame it on natural forces such as pollution, or on supernatural forces. Some Guatemalan villages believe that infertility is due to cold wombs. So the remedy is hot herbal teas or sweat baths. If the infertility is divine in origin, the villagers would not expect these remedies to work, but would seek to atone for the divine punishment by making a sacrifice.

In many societies both Western and Third World, barren women are marginalised, since they are viewed as socially incomplete and personally unfulfilled. Infertility throughout cultures is usually blamed on the female not the man. In one study done in Sri Lanka, it was never acknowledged that men might be the cause of infertility. This mirrors our own problem regarding the recent history of IVF itself (Lee, 1995a; see also Introduction and Chapters 2, 6 and 10).

Somewhere along the path of history, male dominance and male ideology were imposed (Greenstein, 1993), even though there are veiled allusions to female importance in the Bible (God's covenant is with Sarah's blood line and not Abraham's. Furthermore responsibility for a child's religion in the Judaic faith depends on the mother's line). In more modern times, with the rise of the great religions such as Christianity, modern Judaism and Islam, the menstruation time of woman has been used by men as a means of control. It is fascinating to note that most of the great world religions view menstruation as a bad thing. MacCormack & Strathern (eds.), (1980). Either it is a curse put upon women for sin or it is something that can taint men if they come into contact with it. In many societies blood is considered to be a key component regarding how the body works, but it is also considered a pollutant. Menstruation and childbirth have been shrouded in myth as being polluting to men (Gillison, 1980; Goodale, 1980; Strathern, 1980). Whatever the case, as time passed by, a simple physiological act which in fact paves the way for a return to fertility has been ascribed a sinister attribute. This is ironic, since menstruation may actually sometimes be considered positively by both patients and the medical profession when it comes to treatment, since it signals the beginning of a treatment cycle, during which both parties feel hopeful (of course it could also mark the end of a cycle that has failed).

Yet in older times the ritual separation of women in some societies during menstruation or childbirth may have had a positive connotation; instead of being dirty and needing to be isolated from men because of their uncleanliness, the separation may have been to allow them time to deal with their own needs; for rest, being able to get away from physical chores. Women living in close proximity tend to menstruate at the same time. Planned cyclicity may have had a positive use in providing society with a monthly structure. It is possible that women in the distant past were considered to have too much influence, hence the present interpretation of things. Perhaps female power is and was too dangerous to men. Bloch

& Bloch (1980) certainly subscribe to the idea that woman was '... dangerous because of her uncontrolled power and as potentially polluting and disruptive'. Gillison (1980) who carried out field studies on the Gimi people of Papua New Guinea found that in this society women were also seen as polluting. Furthermore, as mentioned in Chapter 1, men may also secretly be jealous of women's ability to bear children. This jealousy along with the other elements discussed above may have resulted in men's need to dominate and subjugate women.

Indeed, although males hold most of the key decision-making roles, they acknowledge a significant fear of women. This fear of women is well founded, since the Gimi have myths concerning ownership of flutes (male phalli), which legend says originally belonged to women. This fits in with Greenstein's (1993) theory that in ancient times women ruled and that men, through greater physical strength were able to usurp their roles and assume a position of dominance to this day. Although he also agrees that man's day may well be up.

Male ideology stems mainly from the idea of hierarchy and results in patriarchy. The Bible draws strongly on such ideas. Abraham's willingness to sacrifice Isaac indicates his willingness (sacrifice on the mount) to carry out his God's instruction in order to gain reward for obedience (duty above all else). The reward is to be ruler; to have rule over land, animals and *women*. It is interesting to look at a woman's response to being told to sacrifice her child. In the story of King Solomon's judgement, the mother would rather give up her child than allow the child to be killed. Compare this with Abraham's willingness to sacrifice Isaac.

Through male ideology men are willing to undergo great suffering, often in silence. The idea of duty lies strongly in men, especially so in the Western world. Duty encompasses the stiff upper lip and the unwritten code that men do not cry. This ideology has served men well for many years through many civilisations but now as we approach the millennium, this ideology is no longer appropriate and is indeed currently partly responsible for men's increasing disarray (Greenstein, 1993). Women are beginning to assert themselves and this new fertility cult is threatening to men, even though it has brought about a reproduction revolution that has exploited women, according to the feminists (Corea, 1985; Scutt, 1990).

For me, the analogy is a fitting one. Infertility clinics essentially assume the role of a modern Messianic legacy. This legacy has produced a phenomenal explosion in the provision of infertility treatments (albeit almost entirely in the private sector). In IVF terms alone, this has meant an increase in IVF/GIFT from ~ 10 000 in 1985 to 20 000 in 1993, effectively a reproduction revolution. In terms of general hospital treatments, these have increased from 20 000 in 1985 to 60 000 non-IVF/GIFT treatment cycles in 1993, hence also the explosion in twin and triplet pregnancies. The number of IVF clinics has also increased from 15 in 1985 to over 100 in 1993.

Undoubtedly, the explosion in availability of IVF is a remarkable phenomenon, a reproduction revolution. The more remarkable, because for the first time ever, the emergence of this new fertility cult actually promotes reproduction without sex. A number of issues arise here. For instance, why are we reinforcing reproduction without sex in clinics? What value are samples produced by masturbation? If we bemoan reproduction without sex, would it not be better to allow couples to produce semen samples through coitus? What is going on here? The reproduction revolution is all about technology (see Fig. 8.2). Technology has heightened people's reproductive desires and hence expectations, as well as changing future possibilities regarding our

Figure 8.2 *Symbolic collage depicting society, religion and Western culture's current reliance on technology.* Modern life has changed to such an extent that many of our cultural roles and rituals have become eroded and consequently unstable. This has led to widespread 'displacement', resulting in the appearance of a fertility cult which relies on the production of children through technology. This modern version of a fertility cult is rooted in religion, technology and money.

When counselling patients, we must always be aware of our own backgrounds, culture and beliefs. It is important to take these factors into consideration when dealing with patients with different beliefs and cultural heritages.

Western kinship system, since we are assisting not only in the making of persons, but also in the making of parents (Strathern, 1992). The price is loss of control as technology assumes the reins and we almost give in completely to any aspect of human desire regarding reproduction. In a way, although most infertility clinics are exploiting a new class of consumer, because reproduction technology extends choices and possibilities for people previously left in limbo (Strathern, 1992), fertility treatment, especially if it works, assumes the guise of a free gift. The free gift is a symbol of modern Western society and as such creates an infinite appetite for what is on offer (Strathern 1992), such as treatment, which has perhaps come to represent one of 'modern times' ultimate manifestations of consumerism (the baby supermarket).

Therefore, those providing treatment, embryologists and especially gynaecologists have become the new high priests and priestesses of temples (infertility clinics) dedicated to the modern-day Messiah, an abstract entity (the new Isis–Osiris) infused with supposed fertility power residing in modern IVF clinics, to those desperately seeking children (Horus) by these means. Many of these couples therefore come to these modern temples of fertility to achieve redemption from their sins (guilt and punishment) by paying for their treatment (equates to sacrifice and atonement). With man generally in crisis, these times are ideally suited for mankind to go in search of a modern Messiah in order to fulfil its expectations of salvation whether it be spiritual or in the context that we are discussing in this book, the desire to have children. The approaching millennium of Aquarius seems to lend itself easily to the sort of changes in society that have been discussed in this chapter. Witness too the tremendous growth of the alternative medicine market.

The church, infertility and treatments

With religion seeming to be such an important issue in our modern temples (IVF clinics), a consideration of the Roman Catholic Church and its views on its new rival is worthwhile. Stone (1990) describes the Catholic point of view. Undoubtedly the Catholic faith of today faces great changes. Increasingly, there is debate on a number of issues, for example on abortion, on issues of priests becoming involved in politics in unstable countries in South America. Nevertheless, one quarter of the world remains faithful in principle to the Roman Catholic Church.

Singer and Wells (1984) looked at the Papal attitude towards infertility treatment. They found that, in spite of the principle that the cornerstone of any marriage is the responsibility of every married couple to procreate, the Church's attitude to infertility treatment is that it represents 'a rupturing of the conjugal act'. Indeed in 1982, Pope John Paul II said the following to a gathering of biologists at the Vatican: '...I condemn, in the most explicit and formal way, experimental manipulation of the human embryo, since the human being, from conception to death, cannot be exploited for any purpose whatsoever'. Quite clearly, IVF is out of the question as far as the Pope is concerned. Not only is the Church against IVF, it also opposes experimentation, freezing and eugenics.

The Church views collection of semen by masturbation as a 'disordered act', whilst DI is viewed as being 'contrary to the dignity of procreation and the conjugal union', which is also how the Pope condemned IVF in 1987 (Congregation for the Doctrine of Faith. *Instruction on respect for human life in its origin and on the dignity of procreation*).

These views deserve some consideration, not because of the church's standpoint, but from the point of view that assisted reproduction treatment (ART) in some cases clearly interferes with some couples' relationships, to such an extent that conjugal union does not take place outside of treatment. Furthermore, IVF itself represents at its most extreme, reproduction without sex.

Religion is even today, far from an irrelevant historical viewpoint. Religions have existed from time immemorial. The USA is currently the land of evangelical Christianity. There are also many brands and sects such as Mormons, Seventh Day Adventists, Moonies, Scientologists and TV evangelists. These which are mostly varying degrees of Christianity all have their own views about infertility and ways of alleviating it. Many of these religions exhibit a fundamental reactionary type of outlook. There is no consensus of opinion in terms of all religions when considering the ethics of treatment. Eastern religions, unlike Western ones have a viewpoint of cyclicity, so arguments tend not to follow Western lines of the soul and procreation. Eastern religions tend to look on life and rebirth which puts a different complexion on life. The cessation of life is actually an escape (in Islam the soul enters the body in the fourth month of pregnancy).

The view of Judaism on infertility treatment and conception

Jakobovits (1990) has described how in the Jewish tradition, as distinct from the Catholic viewpoint (from conception the embryo is human) the embryo has no human rights. The key interpretation separating these two great religions stems from the way a passage in Exodus 21:22 is interpreted. Some discussions have centred on the form of the embryo, for example an embryo with human form is a fetus. Some believe that a fetus is a sacrosanct being (depending on the school in Talmud), others do not. The idea of not 'spilling seed in vain' may be seen as an extension of Onanism (a prohibition on frustrating the procreative act), the obverse of 'go forth and multiply' (Genesis 1:28;9:1). Destruction of an embryo or deliberate wastage of semen or eggs is a grave offence, but not a capital offence or sin. Infertility treatment, because it helps people to comply with the first of the 613 Commandments (go forth and . . ., Genesis 1:28;9:1), is viewed with sympathy, so long as it does not infringe on moral imperatives, such as the sanctity of life, dignity of the individual, inviolability of marriage and its duty of procreation. In IVF, DI or IUI, independent verification (two or more observers) must be undertaken to ensure that no errors are made. There are no moral objections to preimplantation diagnosis (PD) or gene therapy. In general freezing of gametes is proscribed as a repugnant idea. DI and surrogacy are seen as acts which are indefensible violations of rights of the prospective children.

Masturbation

All ART usually requires a male sample to be produced by masturbation. The male must perform to order. Hitherto, until this point in treatment, he has been the neglected unimportant man, playing the role of the partner waiting in the wings. Now he becomes all important and is expected to perform to order. He must produce a sample of semen, usually in the clinic and more often than not, he must produce it on his own, knowing that everyone is waiting expectantly for it. The sample itself takes on a type of symbolism, so that sometimes men are unable to produce it in such difficult circumstances. Perhaps, when the occasion arises, the man is saying something symbolically about ART. Such events, when they occur are hardly surprising, not only are there high stakes riding on the production of the semen sample, but there are also religious aspects as well. To both the Catholic church and Orthodox Judaism, masturbation is an abomination. This may also add a further burden of guilt for many couples. Throughout Africa, amongst Arab countries and other countries in the non-Western world, there may also be taboos against masturbation, which makes this method of semen production even more stressful than it might normally be. This act further exacerbates the removal of sex from ART, perhaps reinforcing the idea of reproduction without sex.

Thus, the requirement of masturbation as a means of the production of the semen sample for use in the treatment ensures patient compliance. It ensures that the laboratory gains access to the sample within an hour of its production, which helps in assessing and preparing the sample for use. It also ensures that couples are not in a position to swap the sample with a known donor. In my experience there are a number of couples who might try the latter given the chance. So part of the reason for masturbation is to maintain the clinic's control over the patient.

> Why do we stop couples from producing by coitus? The simple official answer is that recovering semen from the vagina might be a messy affair.

Samples obtained by interruptus are usually poor. Both these methods are unreliable because semen is made up from the secretion of several glands. The most important emission being that from the epididymis, which is where the sperm are stored just prior to ejaculation. Unfortunately, the emission from the epididymis is the first one, so that by the time the other glands, the prostate, seminal vesicles and the bulbourethral glands have also emitted, the first portion may be already widely dispersed (first portion is only about 0.5 ml, whereas the rest may be 2 to 8 ml). Thus even with interruptus, we usually only get the fluid from the accessory glands rather than the epididymis, which has been left behind in the vagina. So, to summarise, samples produced by sex, for treatment purposes are likely to be of poor quality, unless we collect into a seminal device; a device which must be non toxic and non spermicidal. Such devices exist and indeed, most men are able to produce through coitus into these devices. Why do we not routinely use these devices? I am not sure. I am aware that embryologists have some reluctance about handling the devices (most are female, which might explain this?) and there may be issues of cost (£5–10 per device), but at the end of the day, it could be about patient control and compliance. A researcher, Zavos (1985) has studied the use of these devices extensively in the USA. He has carried out a number of studies which show that semen samples produced with the devices are improved over samples produced by the same men through masturbation. Some of the studies are possibly flawed, but the implication is that masturbation semen samples may be suboptimal, begging the question, if we assume masturbation produces poor samples, of how meaningful is IVF failure to fertilise? Is it possible that such cases might be reversed if we were to obtain a further sample from coitus using a seminal device to catch the whole sample? It is a moot and ironic point. More research needs to be done. Almost certainly there are benefits to be obtained from the use of such devices, with the only risk being that some couples might swap samples on us.

Ethnic factors

D'Ardenne & Mahtani (1989) have suggested that, whereby in the past, most counsellors have tended to stick to clients from their own back-grounds, society is changing sufficiently quickly so that increasingly in the future, counsellors are going to be faced more and more with clients whose ethnic background is likely to be very different. They believe that counsellors must therefore begin to adopt a flexible approach and that it is important to be aware of our own potential prejudices and stereo-typing towards others. If we as counsellors do not address these issues, we make the counsellor–client relationship unbalanced. This serves to place the counsellor in an even stronger position of power over the client. Even in client-centred counselling with persons from the same background as ourselves the client is often in a slightly disadvantaged position. In their book, d'Ardenne and Mahtani have concentrated on four cases, two involving cross-cultural counselling. On the grounds of the cases presented they have built up a model, whereby they feel it is important to find a common language. In cross-cultural situations there are three distinct barriers, language, class values and culture bound values (Atkinson *et al.*, 1983). Language has to be considered in both verbal and non-verbal terms. When considering class, we should bear in mind that traditionally counselling is oriented towards the upper and middle classes. Some classes (lower middle and working) particularly value the giving of advice and immediate solutions. With respect to culture, we need to be aware of the differences between counsellor and client, particularly with regard to ethnic minorities (Vantress, 1986).

Sue Jennings (1988) has been instrumental in pointing out how different people perceive medical matters differently, according to their cultural heritage and ethnic backgrounds. Not every culture shares the same value systems, attitudes and beliefs about the human body, its dysfunctions and cures. It is important for us in the Western world to realise that when dealing with someone from a different culture, particularly with a different ethnic background, that we must learn to understand their 'language' in order that we might understand their symptoms properly, be absolutely clear about the diagnosis, and ascertain properly what they have understood about the problem and what may be done for it. For example, Jennings (1988) reports the following anecdote: 'You'll have to take it out of me doctor. It's no good' (a cry from a woman for an incision to let out the badness in her, as is customary in the medical system of her own culture, rather than an appeal for an hysterectomy!).

When considering class values, Jennings has described the following: Gypsies are considered by most people to be dirty, yet gypsies judge the cleanliness of their neighbours by the gap on the washing line between their knickers and the tea towels.

We must be careful of imposing our own values. Take for instance sex selection (Lee, 1993). Certain cultures such as those in India and China value male children very highly. In Western culture, we see such desires as being 'unnatural' and in the main undesirable (Lee, 1993); however, as seen in Case History 8.1, for some couples it is very important.

Case history 8.1

Mr and Mrs AA came to the clinic for a consultation regarding their desire to have a male child. My own prejudices against sex selection are well known (Lee, 1993), nevertheless, the couple had been referred to me by a friend, who thought that both the clients and I might benefit from meeting. Mr AA was very depressed. He was a successful business man from Calcutta. The couple already had two daughters (seen in Indian culture as

> **Case history 8.1** *continued*
>
> very much other people's wives and also as a potential drain on family resources with respect to the dowry that must be paid when they are wed). Mr AA felt that his society expected him to have a male heir and that great shame was attached to him if he failed.
>
> Mrs AA was fearful that if she did not provide him with a male heir that he would leave her and that this would place great shame on herself and her family. (I began to understand that not only was there shame on the couple but also shame on the families that each of the clients derived from.)

In such a case as that above, we are dealing with a cultural conundrum, so many aspects are in opposition to each other. It certainly took a great deal of restraint to avoid imposing my own values on the couple. Their belief in their own right and the absolute necessity of their desire was unmistakably resolute. Nothing was going to change their mind nor their intent. At the end of the day, I affirmed their beliefs and their decision to seek a solution, though I had to regrettably explain to them that there was no obvious medical solution. One possibility was ultrasound scanning at about 13–15 weeks of pregnancy, but this method is unreliable and would involve a highly undesirable termination of pregnancy. Another possibility might have been to consult the London Gender Clinic in Hendon, which provides an 'unproven' method of insemination (Lee, 1993).

Staying with the theme of culture, it is notable that with Asian families, obligations are very strong and there is a tremendous restraint of emotions. This culture places high value on achievement and a strong sense of shame and guilt pervade each and every family within a community. These cultural values are almost always used as control measures. We must also be aware of our own tendency to racism. When considering African culture, it is important to bear in mind their shared past history of exploitation and suppression. Here in the West, as with Asians, Africans also suffer from prejudice and discrimination. Tribally they have strong kinship bonds and often exhibit an adaptability of family roles (MacCormack & Strathern (ed.), 1980). In particular Africans may exhibit conflicted cultural roles as many have adopted Western religious orientations, even though they may still be steeped in their own indigenous religions and non-Western medical traditions.

Native American Indians have a strong concept of sharing and show tremendous resilience in adversity. They possess a stoic humour rather than pessimism and exhibit a high degree of inner serenity. They are a stoic race and are extremely patient (Atkinson *et al.*, 1983).

In the previous paragraph, we examine some generalisations concerning different ethnic groups on different continents. It is important nevertheless for us to avoid stereotyping people and to avoid prejudice, an irrational attitude of behaviour towards any person or group or their supposed characteristics. People displaced and in different cultures from their origin, experience the following: *conformity*, because of discrimination, there is a tendency for appreciation (change) towards the dominant culture; *dissonance*, a conflict between one's own feeling of worth involving both resistance and immersion in the new culture; *introspection*, a tendency to immerse oneself in one's own former culture. Counsellors need to bear all the above in mind and it is important also to remember that displaced persons need to develop an ability to hold themselves in high self esteem and to keep their original culture as well as being able to draw effectively from their new culture. Within this context many skills used by counsellors, for example, eye contact, disclosures, verbalisation, are perhaps not useful.

Finally, let us consider the Western medical model which is paternalistic. We no longer pay attention to folk health, although there are some who adhere stringently to popular healthcare methods, nowadays represented by the fringe so-called alternative/complementary medicine. Here too we can explore cross-cultural attitudes and beliefs in relation to medicine and how different cultures perceive illness and health. In different cultures, different foods are considered as healthy or unhealthy. Certain foods may be seen as medicinal, certain as celebratory food. We must also be aware of differences in outlook about such matters as menstruation, masturbation, sexual intercourse, conception and childbirth, infertility and treatment. We should therefore always be looking for conflicts between treatment and religious, ethical and cultural beliefs.

Conclusion

The contents of this chapter are meant to illustrate how we owe many of our beliefs and attitudes to issues which have been handed down to us through the ages (sometimes crossing millennia) and it is hoped will serve to demonstrate the pervasive influence that religions, both modern and ancient, have on our thinking about fertility. Other issues dealt with here centre on both cultural and ethnic influences on how we look at fertility and medicine itself.

Once again, I am intrigued at how the issues of guilt and punishment seem to have cropped up in several chapters. Whether these issues are rooted in religion, psychology, culture or ethnic background is unclear. What seems certain is that these issues are very powerful and with regard to fertility and those who are infertile, they may be two of the most important feelings, which if dealt with effectively may have important repercussions in couples' expectations, desires and treatment outcome. Consequently, worked through the threads of the contents of this long and difficult chapter are the themes of: crisis, Western people's need for a new Messiah, rebirth and resurrection, a cult of children and the emergence therefore of a new fertility cult centred on IVF clinics, the issue of guilt and punishment leading to couples needing to pay for treatment in order to be redeemed, which thereby allows them to become reborn as parents of a child (Horus) 'gifted' to them by the modern temples of the cult of fertility, of which the priests and high priestesses are the embryologists and gynaecologists.

Chapter 9
Donor Insemination and Male Infertility

Introduction

Donor insemination (DI) is a common method used to overcome infertility in the male (see Snowden & Snowden, 1993). It is most suitable in cases of irreversible azoospermia. Often, it is also used to treat couples in whom the male partner has oligozoospermia, asthenozoospermia and oligoasthenozoospermia (see Fig. 9.1). In my opinion,

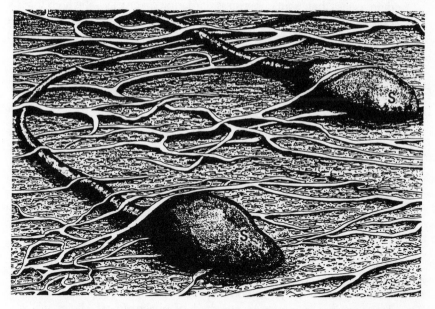

Figure 9.1 *Donor sperms are meant to be the best.* This figure shows a good donor sperm, marked (**S**) moving purposefully through cervical mucus. Donor insemination requires the recruitment of donors. These donors are usually men aged between 18 and 25 years. In the UK their identity is kept anonymous. Not all donor semen in use is proven (only 50% in use at any one time) and good donors are only allowed a maximum of ten pregnancies in the UK after which they must be replaced. Features of the prospective male patient are matched as closely as possible regarding eye colour, build, height, hair colour, complexion, etc.

probably only the oligoasthenozoospermics (and those with very severe oligozoospermia: less than 5 million per ml; and asthenozoospermia: less than 5% motility) are *bona fide* patients for DI, in addition to azoospermics.

DI has been practised in its modern form since the 1930s (although it is believed that physicians in ancient Egypt also practised it), though until the 1960s it was definitely behind closed doors. In recent years, DI has become more commonplace and is currently an accepted method for overcoming male infertility, when adoption is not considered as an option. Often critics have pointed out that because DI's roots lay in the world of animal husbandry (bovine in particular), those taking part were guilty of practising human husbandry, and were reducing human procreation to a stockyard practice. Gina Corea (1985), author of the book *Mother Machine*, sees much that is bad with regard to DI. Her image of DI certainly relates to the idea of animal husbandry, since in her book she offers the reader a long commentary on her own observations on how DI is done in the USA on cattle. She obviously viewed the procedure as less than gentle, perhaps bordering on cruelty. She feels that DI on humans is not so very different. The idea of DI as an abomination is further enhanced for her when she considers the idea of the Nobel Sperm Bank, set up in 1976, as a further step towards eugenics.

Recent changes, the HFEA and current practices in modern DI

As already mentioned in Chapter 2, formerly (pre-1985) prior to clinics becoming more scrupulous with regard to potential diseases in semen, donor insemination was done with both fresh and frozen semen. Partly because of the advent of AIDS, most clinics had moved towards a frozen system by 1987, since the use of frozen specimens allows for semen testing and quarantine. All samples are therefore now frozen and stored before use. This allows both the serum of the donor and the semen sample to be AIDS tested. Nevertheless, the frozen sample may not be used until another 3 to 6 months have elapsed and a second serum sample from the donor has proved to be HIV negative. This does not of course guarantee that all donor samples are totally disease free, but at least ensures a minimum standard of quality (most clinics will also genetically screen the samples as well as testing for common microbiological contaminants). The use of frozen semen samples in DI thus ensures improved quality control and quality assurance for patients.

Donors themselves are also subject to greater controls since 1987 than previously. Pre-1980, donors could donate at many clinics and it was hard to know how many children a donor might have sired. Now, any donor is allowed a maximum of ten successes, after which he may no longer be a donor. Donors are also subject to tighter selection criteria. In the UK and most of Europe and in the USA, donors are guaranteed anonymity, whereas in Sweden donors may be identified. Initially, donors almost disappeared there, but presently supply just about matches demand. Whether this system would work elsewhere is debatable. In France, couples are encouraged to introduce a donor, but their own treatment must involve an anonymous donor.

Even though donor clinics are under close scrutiny, and in the UK since 1990 they have been under the regulating authority of the HFEA, treatment may still be somewhat haphazard. For instance, my own experience of clinics is that up to 50% of donors used do not have proven capability. Furthermore, some donors rapidly reach the point where they may not be used any more, whilst some may still be in use after over 300 treatment cycles. It should also be borne in mind that even today, according to the latest HFEA data, the average DI clinic is only achieving a delivery rate of 5% per treatment cycle, considerably lower than the poor IVF success rates. In my opinion, part of the explanation for the poor results lies in the use of frozen–thawed samples (freezing and thawing greatly affects the ability of sperm to penetrate cervical mucus), and the problem may be overcome by the use of sperm preparation as per IVF and the use of IUI (see also Chapter 3).

Donor semen and IVF or GIFT

The use of donor samples is not just restricted to DI, but its use in IVF or GIFT is also common. How does this come about? There are a significant number of couples where the female partners, who have patent tubes, persistently fail DI treatment. Eventually these couples may, with their agreement, progress on to GIFT or IVF. Equally so, there are couples who need IVF because the female partner has blocked tubes (see Case History 9.1). As a consequence of the IVF, these couples might serendipitiously discover that the male partner is also subfertile (failed or poor fertilisation). These couples are then likely to continue with donor-IVF. The third group are couples with male partners known to have sub-optimal semen quality. These couples initially have IVF as a test of sperm function. After several cycles with poor fertilisation, they may then be persuaded to consider the donor option, perhaps initially as a half and half option (half eggs with husband, etc.) or with GIFT, donor sperm in one tube and husband's on the other. After a while, these couples may finally elect to have donor-IVF only (in which case, they might be better off considering DI with IUI rather than further IVF).

Case history 9.1

Mr and Mrs J wished to be counselled because they were considering IVF with donor semen. Mr J was born with congenital absence of *vas defe-rens* and so was azoospermic. The couple needed IVF because Mrs J also had blocked tubes. Bearing in mind the blocked tubes, the couple spent part of one session exploring the bitterness of having DI treatment in a Wimpole Street clinic. The issue of wasted time, hope and money seemed to weigh heavily on their minds.

Mr J is very stoic and a typical private person. Mrs J says he never cuddles her and always behaves in a restrained manner, even when they are alone. No one knows about the treatment. Neither family nor friends. If the treatment is successful, they will keep the whole thing secret, unto the grave if possible.

They saw the IVF treatment with donor semen as a last option. Mr J stated that he was getting old (he is 45 years old, whilst she is 38) and that he felt it was almost time to call it a day. If the attempts at IVF failed he wished to close the book on the matter.

Social and psychological attitudes to DI

Let us now consider some of the information that social and psychological research has thrown up. Oldereid, Rui & Purvis (1991) have found increasingly negative attitudes to DI. Some 20% of he men who had submitted to DI treatment had also sought fringe medicine solutions. Perhaps indicating that even when men agree to participate in DI, they still hold out some hope for miracles. In my own work, I can confirm this. A good many of the couples that attend my andrology clinic are long-standing infertility patients. Often, through some tenuous path they have alighted on the clinic and are present to seek a third, fourth, fifth or even sixth opinion as to their situation. Some freely admit that they are desperate for some news, such as new advances which will be relevant to their infertility. Over the years, I am afraid, I have usually had to disappoint them.

Van Thiel *et al.* (1990) surprisingly found that with DI most psychological reactions were found in the female partner. They feared loss of respect from their peers and relatives. They feared rejection also from their partners, whom they thought might see the donor as a rival (a common reaction, but they also fear that the prospective child may also be seen as a rival for affection). The men on the other hand were unable to acknowledge their sterility (as mentioned elsewhere in this book, men get stuck at this stage of denial), being ambivalent and seemingly fearful of castration anxiety. Men also clearly feared being excluded by their partners, many volunteering the idea that they felt potentially threatened by the mother–child relationship; this acknowledgement too is very common (Lee, unpublished observation), see Case History 9.2).

Case history 9.2

Mr and Mrs P were counselled because Mr P was feeling rather anxious about the impending DI treatment. Mr P had a very dry sense of humour and after careful exploration concerning his azoospermia, it seemed clear that he was reasonably at peace with his infertility.

During the counselling, it became clear that Mrs P was the main driving force behind the DI option. Nevertheless, Mr P was happy to proceed, but harboured a number of fears. The worst being that the prospective DI child 'might drive a wedge between us', as he put it. There were other issues, for instance, he was also worried that he might not be able to love the child as if it was his own.

Ideally, Mr P would have preferred to adopt. However, because of scarcity and age (both were over 35 years old), this was the least possible option. At the end of the day, Mr P got the chance to 'let off steam' about the DI. Mr and Mrs P had the opportunity to speak frankly to each other about the treatment. In spite of his fears, Mr P was able to proceed (in a presentation to the British Psychological Society in 1994, S. Golombok demonstrated that her study of DI parents showed that couples who had children by means of DI made good parents).

Klock & Maier (1992) found that 81% of couples who had told others about their having DI treatment regretted doing so. If there was a next time, they stated, they would not do so again. Furthermore they found that 86% had not and would not tell the prospective child about its true origins. These findings are consistent with my own experiences; during implications counselling, I always explore the issue of 'keeping things secret' or not. We explore the range of possibilities and how things can go wrong, particularly when secrecy is a strong issue. From work done at the Rowan Clinic at the Royal London Hospital and the Hale Clinic, I find that 90% of couples indicate a desire to keep 'things' secret (see Case History 9.1).

Schover, Collins & Richards (1992) showed that when couples were subjected to psychological assessments, the psychologist's rating correlated with pregnancy outcome. In other words, where the rating was 'Excellent' the couples' success rate was 59%, whereas those scored as 'At risk' only had a success rate of 14%. The same authors (Schover, Rothmann & Collins, 1992) also found that 70% of male donors were motivated by money. Additionally 35% were prone to alcohol abuse. Compared to women donors, men were assessed as being much less altruistic. On the other hand it was found that female donors tended to have traumatic family and reproductive histories.

Cross-cultural differences in the experience of DI might also be useful. Savage (1992) has shown that in Yaounde in Africa, only 19.6% of men would undertake DI. Most male respondents did not perceive DI as an acceptable alternative to infertility in this society. Here in the UK, in contrast, Owens, Edelmann & Humphrey (1993) found that about 65% of men were happy to consider DI. A total of 205 couples were included in the study. About one third resolved their infertility, of these 36 by DI success and 28 by adoption. Spontaneous success was rare. In keeping with reports mentioned earlier in this chapter, few (26%) decided to tell the child if they were successful with DI.

Other issues concerning DI

In 1991 there was a furore concerning what is known as Virgin Birth Syndrome (VBS) (Silman, 1993). In itself, there seems little of relevance to this book. However, a number of issues were raised at a symposium on the matter, which was held at the Royal London Hospital in 1992. The two key questions were as follows:

(1) Are donors sowing wild oats?
(2) What is the incentive of donors?

The reason VBS was relevant to DI is that those 'so-called' virgins who were seeking to have children wanted to do so through DI treatment. The questions raised above came to the fore when those arguing for access to DI for persons with so-called VBS questioned the motives of male sperm donors. The motives are certainly relevant, and most studies have found that the majority of donors are not just altruists; since they almost all expect some form of payment for expenses. The question of wild oats is also relevant. On this matter there is less information, but whilst there may be a number of donors who wish to test their fertility, etc., this is likely to be a lesser issue. Certainly a donor who admits to this may be less likely to be accepted as a donor. The idea of VBS is also frightening to men, since their worst fears, when looking into future images of DI, is that men might become redundant if all women choose to have children by DI (see Chapter 1).

A common fear in infertility clinics is that somehow semen samples might be mixed up and the wrong sample would be placed into the wrong patient. Whilst this is not the fear in a DI clinic, the USA furore over a practitioner, Jacobsen, who is alleged to have sired over 19 so-called DI babies, highlights a common fantasy in patients. This is certainly the stuff of much innuendo here in the UK. Many DI patients often jokingly mention the idea that perhaps the sample they are receiving might belong not to sperm donors but to men working in the clinic themselves. Happily, I am sure that this is a very rare possibility indeed, but it does not stop couples from continuing to fantasise about it.

The paragraph concerning VBS may be considered to highlight an area where DI might be involved in a growth industry. If we dismiss the issue over virgins, there may in the future be more and more single women wishing to start or complete families without the need to indulge in sexual relationships. As society changes and women become more powerful and independent it is likely that the emphasis of DI treatment may move somewhat away from male infertility treatment, to offering independent women further reproductive options than they used to have (Strathern, 1992). Indeed the technology may have many more spin-offs. Couples taking part in surrogacy arrangements (where one woman offers to carry a pregnancy on behalf of another couple) with or without donor eggs may also choose to use donor sperm. The possible permutations are endless.

Donor insemination and counselling: implications

Before finishing this chapter, we must look at implications counselling for donor insemination. When counselling men and couples who are considering or who have chosen to have DI, there are a number of issues which must be explored. One should bear in mind that with DI, once again, the treatment centres on the woman despite the problem lying with the man. So even with DI, the man is marginalised, feels useless and is in many ways isolated. As well as dealing with the implications of DI, it is also an opportunity for the man to explore his feelings regarding his plight. These feelings have been discussed extensively already. It is also pertinent to explore a man's feelings regarding DI itself (see Case History 9.3). Some men arrive easily at the decision, but most men agonise over the decision. Some men are highly resistant to the idea, but eventually acquiesce. In my experience DI is often initiated as an option by the female partner, in contrast to the scenario of IVF with the husband's poor semen. It is rare for the man to have to persuade his partner to take up DI treatment. (There are also situations when the female partner may ask for DI treatment to be kept *secret from her partner*.) The vast majority of men have grave reservations about DI, although they may agree to accept the treatment. However, despite the reservations it is clear that when the decision is made, it is always made in an optimistic manner and is often viewed as a 'gift' for their partner.

Case history 9.3

Mr and Mrs H attended for counselling regarding the implications of DI. Mr H had been shocked by his diagnosis of severe asthenozoospermia. He had felt that it was unfair and had been upset enough to cry. He had also been very angry, but felt that he was past that now. His own family was large and all his siblings had children. He felt very guilty about his infertility and he felt he was to blame. He had suggested several times to Mrs H that she should find someone else.

They had tried to tell friends and family about the DI, but felt that they were unlikely to broach the subject any more with them. They would not make a secret of the DI if they were lucky enough to succeed (one of the few couples I have found willing to share the information). They knew that life would change greatly if they had a child. Mrs H surprisingly showed regret about this. She wistfully stated that apart from the child-lessness, they currently led very pleasant and comfortable lives, often going out and partying. They also acknowledged that they might well find it hard to make ends meet, but were very happy to make sacrifices.

He did not have any fantasies regarding the prospective child (evidence of reluctance?), whilst she did and felt that it would fulfil a life ambition if the DI worked. They were indeed worried about treatment failure and felt that the future was very uncertain as well as saying that they felt the nature of the treatment was very haphazard. Mr H showed further indications of anxiety regarding the DI, when we explored the possibility of a large family through DI. Mrs H was enthusiastic and volunteered to have four children. Mr H immediately interjected and became highly agitated (arms waving wildly) and suggested that they would decide after the first one if they were lucky.

When challenged about his apparent ambivalence to the DI treatment, Mr H stated that he was resolved regarding his infertility, but did find it hard coming to terms with DI at times. He stated a few times that he had nothing to hide (unsolicited denial) and that although he would prefer to have 'my own child', he could live with the DI option. In a way, he admitted that he was doing it mainly for Mrs H. It was important for her so likewise it was important to him also.

During implications counselling, it is important to consider the clients' own feelings about DI and the prospective child. They have to consider possible changes in their financial, social and psychological circumstances. They must consider their own families. How will their families feel about DI? Indeed, will the respective families be told? Couples must consider whether they will keep the DI a secret. If they choose this option, they must consider the likely complications and problems. In my experience, up to 90% (see above) of all couples considering DI will wish to keep the treatment a secret (limited to close family only, often to man and wife only). They must also consider the needs of the prospective, unborn child. The welfare of the child is of paramount importance. Unusually, here counsellors are expected to take action if they feel that the prospective (as yet unconceived) child is in any danger (presumably from abuse?). Under such circumstances, one assumes the couple might be barred from treatment should the doubts prove to be substantiated. It is also worth pointing out that a couple must consider that treatment may not necessarily succeed. This is one area where counselling is prescribed. It is a significant part of the code of practice regarding the Human Fertilisation and Embryology Act of 1990.

As a final footnote to this section, we should bear in mind that the use of donor semen and indeed male infertility itself, in certain circumstances can lead to emotional difficulties. The stresses and strains of treatment may lead to failed marriages or even the termination of pregnancy following successful treatment outcome. The careful use and availability of skilled counselling should ensure that these sad outcomes will be minimised.

Conclusion

Modern donor insemination, as a treatment (and as a social psychological phenomenon) has come a long way since its early days, when it was compared to animal husbandry. Much of its transformation to being an acceptable form of infertility treatment has depended on the reproduction revolution, but we should not discount some of the other social changes (which also helped to bring about the revolution in reproduction). Throughout the 1940s, 1950s, 1960s, 1970s, 1980s and now the 1990s, western society has undergone great change. One very significant change in making DI much more socially acceptable is the fact that clinics are now regulated by the HFEA. This means that DI has now entered the realms of authentication, good laboratory practice and quality assurance. Already, a number of DI clinics have ceased to trade and there is some evidence of DI coming under the umbrella of mainstream IVF clinics, perhaps as a consequence of the HFEA or perhaps this was a shakeup waiting to happen and precipitated by a new burden of licensing fees and the cost of administration (licensing and being licensed involves a great deal of bureaucracy since every treatment cycle must now be reported on in detail and filed with the HFEA). The future evolution of DI is only beginning to take shape and it will certainly be interesting to see what ICSI will do to the field as it becomes established and more widely available.

Interestingly, although it is and has always been an option in cases of male infertility, DI actually strikes at the very core of a man's existence, which makes its acceptance that much more of a sacrifice on the man's part than might at first be apparent. The fact that many DI children have been born and in spite of the father's worries, anxieties and fears; DI appears to have been a successful (not in the meaning of success rates; recent data reported by Professor S. Golombok at a British Psychology Society conference in 1994) method of being a pathway to pregnancy for many couples who were willing to explore a modern version of semi-social parenting. This is all the more remarkable, since male ideology mitigates against social parenting. Perhaps it is these men (and their type) who are able somehow to overcome their male ideology imprinting, and to emerge from the trauma, isolation, denial and marginalisation of their plight, having shown themselves able to turn depression and adversity into an act filled with optimism, who will adapt best to the social changes ahead.

Chapter 10
The Medical Agenda

Introduction

An excursion into history may be most useful at the beginning of this chapter. The profession of medicine was dominated by female healers in Europe until the sixteenth century. Women's problems at this time period in particular were dealt with by women. However, in the witch hunts of the sixteenth and seventeenth centuries, the balance was redressed, so that by the nineteenth century, medicine was a profession dominated by men. This seems to mimic the general scenario of female power having been usurped by men in the very distant past of human history (Gillison, 1980; Greenstein, 1993). So dominant was the male patriarchy that it was not till the mid nineteenth century in the UK that the first woman doctor, Elizabeth Garrett Anderson, qualified. Similar circumstances existed in the USA and many other parts of Europe. This is therefore the background for both USA and Europe in how medicine and gynaecology in particular came to be male dominated. Consequently and paradoxically, infertility investigations and treatment have concentrated on the woman, thereby leaving the investigation of men behind and the study of male infertility in the dark ages.

Over the years as men gained ascendancy over women in the field of obstetrics it is interesting to note that the thin edge of the wedge was the routine use of forceps (Fig. 10.1) and other surgical instruments, to which female midwives were denied access. These instruments therefore gave men for the first time some control over the act of birth. Women were considered to be too illogical, hysterical and unpredictable to be competent to serve as obstetricians. Indeed myths that women were physiologically and psychologically inferior to men were perpetuated by medicine of the day, which by now was male dominated (Jordanova, 1980). Furthermore, there were gynaecologists at this time who believed that female hysteria and other mental disorders might be overcome by clitoridectomy and hysterectomy. With the advent of ART and IVF, this early access to innovation has developed to the point where women are now subject to male culture from conception to birth.

121

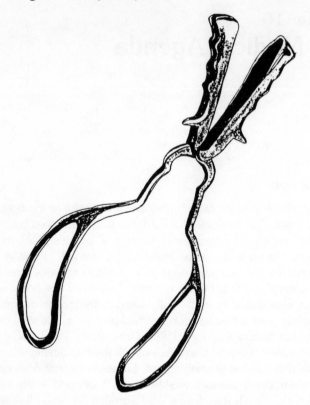

Figure 10.1 *Forceps, symbol of male domination in obstetrics.* The forceps symbolise one of the paradoxes of the medical agenda. The current lack of male infertility specialists is paradoxically mirrored by the lack of female consultant gynaecologists. In the Middle Ages, women were very much involved at the core of the practice of medicine. However, in the seventeenth and eighteenth centuries, medicine became a male preserve. So much so that women wishing to practise medicine had to pose as men. Hence the dominance of men, even in the discipline of gynaecology, which has also led to a dearth of male infertility specialists, because traditionally, infertility specialists are gynaecologists, who by discipline and training have chosen to specialise in women's medicine and surgery.

The feminist perspective

Feminist writers therefore, such as Naomi Pfeffer, feel that patriarchally dominated medicine, especially that discipline of gynaecology, exists to exploit women. Finkelstein (1990) and Scutt (1990) echo these feelings. Their viewpoints suggest that social stereotyping of woman has led to the idea of women predominantly as child bearers. This is seen as a state of constraint and confinement (interestingly also an obstetric medical term). In the past, women without child, husband or domestic duties were viewed with pity. Anyone shunning the pity became a social pariah and was often subjected to medical treatment and surgery. The advent of anaesthetics in the nineteenth century meant that surgical intervention became common as a means of dealing with women's problems. Various types of surgery were promoted (by male surgeons, since there were few female surgeons until the twentieth century) as means of dealing with disorders and the disturbances in women's social roles and behaviour. The twentieth century brought slightly better understanding of women (as well as more female clinicians), whereby female independence no longer meant hysteria or illness related to the womb; instead, just as women were previously treated for social distemper, now the medical profession saw itself as offering women medical treatment to alleviate their condition of childlessness, amongst other disorders. In this way medicine now saw itself benefiting women, by helping them achieve the fulfilment expected of them by modern society.

According to feminist viewpoints (Corea, 1985; Finkelstein, 1990; Koval & Scutt, 1990; Scutt, 1990) fears about over-population have led to further incursions into the reproductive rights of women. Control by the medical profession over births, birth control, abortion, sterilisation and contraception has meant that medical practitioners have become immensely powerful (Corea, 1985; Finkelstein, 1990; Koval & Scutt, 1990; Pfeffer, 1987; Scutt, 1990). Formal medicine is therefore deemed to have cast woman in the narrow role of mother only. Accordingly, women must therefore learn to value pregnancy, birth and family. Medicine (perhaps inadvertently) has reinforced the idea that woman's biological destiny is reproduction. The advent of new reproductive technologies has therefore resulted in further incursions into female rights, as greater control over woman's social future is annexed by those who offer medical reproductive assistance to those seeking help in their search for society's values of female fulfilment.

Feminism, a male perspective and appraisal

Some of these arguments are acceptable to men. To some extent, if we accept the feminist viewpoint, it is a terrible indictment of man and most certainly male ideology. Reproductive technologies may have infringed on women's rights, but paradoxically, in the field of reproductive medicine, the men, male partners of women undergoing surgical treatments for infertility have been similarly cast in the role of guinea pig; although rarely in the position of receiving surgery. Nevertheless these men have quietly made their own contribution in one way or another. As I have pointed out elsewhere, these men suffer in silence and isolation (see Chapters 1, 4, 5, 6, 7 and 8). So deep in denial, they function as sperm providers, men required to produce semen on demand so that surgical treatments may go ahead. Lo and behold, should the sperm provider fail to produce a sample, the whole treatment cycle is then at risk. It is surprising that more men do not fail to produce a sample. These neglected men continue to be marginalised by clinics (witness Peter Humm's (1989) autobiographical piece in Chapter 7). It is important that clinics should in future try to involve men much more in the process of diagnosis and treatment. As we involve men more, we may be able to get more men past the isolation phase and thus get more couples to function better as a unit, as they progress through treatment.

The future of ART might represent great possibilities for women. Certainly, as women gain more independence and redress the balance, as the former male ideology is banished to history, a new golden age of reproduction may beckon. Undoubtedly from a feminist perspective, there are obviously a number of issues. However, men who are being treated by men (gynaecologists) who have opted to work on women have a right to feel that they have been the neglected male partner over the years and this needs addressing quickly. The infertile man deserves as much attention as his counterpart.

Why do men become gynaecologists? Why so few women?

Since I have outlined my hypothesis about how male domination in reproductive medicine came about and its consequences regarding men and male infertility, it seems a good idea to explore why the condition persists and how it is propagated. Kutner & Brogan (1990) carried out a study on medical undergraduates in the USA. They found more women were interested in obstetrics and gynaecology than men, but were no more likely to be in such careers when followed up later. It seems that part of the explanation for men's great interest in gynaecology was their desire to be in a surgical speciality. The male obstetrics and gynaecology oriented students were more traditional in their sex roles both as students and as practising doctors, whereas women were much more likely than their male peers to treat their patients in an egalitarian manner. (N.B.: traditional medicine in the West tends to be paternalistic, because most doctors are still male.)

Metheny, Blount & Holzman (1991) also found that more women than men as students elected for obstetrics and gynaecology. Those choosing this profession liked the idea of working with mostly healthy patients and had strong opinions about reproduction issues. Again they were also interested in surgical careers. The future for women in obstetrics and gynaecology is thought to lie in more access for them to structured training. Also more availability of part-time training for women, particularly with reference to women and their roles in nurturing families, even in egalitarian partnerships in marriage.

No better advertisement for women's cause is needed that Sichel's

(1991) comment that there is often difficulty in comprehension between patient and doctor, that the doctor must decode the female code in order to understand the woman's request, by putting aside his personal point of view and his medical code. Therefore a simple solution is to have more female gynaecologists. Both the above studies showed more women interested in the speciality than men, yet why then the male domination? At a meeting on the Calman report (on the need for change in the medical profession by the UK's chief medical officer) at the Royal College of Obstetrics and Gynaecology in 1994, it was pointed out that even now only about 10% of consultants in obstetrics and gynaecology were women. One explanation is that women do not apply for consultant posts, another is that knowing they will be excluded, women do not bother to apply. The true answer still remains a mystery.

Conclusion

I hope it becomes clear from the issues discussed in this chapter that men, as patients, have been ignored. Often in cases of male infertility in the past, the assumption has always been made that the infertility lies with the woman. This has meant that couples have been given months, perhaps years, of treatment before the male partner has been fully investigated, in the past. This potential for abuse lies in the still largely paternalistic outlook of Western medicine. In reproductive medicine, the issue is further exacerbated paradoxically, because in spite of men dominating the field, which should have led to heightened sympathy, options and care for their male patients, fertility specialists, because they have chosen to work on women, are themselves in a strange state of denial, which for many years has led to male infertility being ignored by the profession. As I have pointed out, the appointment of more female consultants in obstetrics and gynaecology is unlikely to help, since women are also part of the conspiracy of silence and neglect (because of the pervasiveness of male ideology), and more importantly, gynaecology is still obviously all about women and not men. Thus there exists a paradox concerning treatment options and feminism, in that technology really does widen female choice.

So in spite of the real exploitation and the use of female bodies as guinea-pigs, the infertility clinics hardly treat men any better, perhaps even worse. In the long run, as technology moves on, as pointed out in Chapters 1 and 7, because of the increased options and choice (Strathern, 1992), women may paradoxically seize the high ground and as our Western kinship system adapts to new images of the future (Strathern, 1992; women having careers and still having children late in life by ovum donation or the freezing and storage of their own eggs and embryos for future use, etc.) it seems to me that men will be in increasing disarray, because the social changes that technology threatens seem to present men with increasing discontinuity and change, whilst women become potentially more empowered. The balance will be redressed after millennia of male dominance (Greenstein, 1993).

The way ahead in terms of the medical agenda is for men and male infertility to be properly addressed. Most importantly, formalised training needs to be set in place for those wishing to practise reproductive medicine, which needs to encompass andrology (male medicine) as well as gynaecology (Philipp, 1984). As men's needs become acknowledged and more training and knowledge is achieved, some of the problems discussed in this chapter and book will begin to diminish. Unfortunately, the problem may take another two to three generations before we see any real change.

Chapter 11
Law, Ethics and Morals of ART

Introduction

The field of ART has generated more than its fair share of controversy over the years. It is even more astonishing since Louise Brown (the UK's first 'test-tube baby') was not born until 1978, just 18 years ago, whilst in the interim we have had more moral issues to deal with than some fields have generated over several centuries (see Corea, 1985; Lee, 1989, 1992, 1993; Scutt, 1990; Strathern 1992). On a day-to-day basis, all of us who work in this field tread a moral and ethical minefield as we deal with many difficult issues such as surrogacy, ovum donation, sex selection, the possible use of fetal tissue (a child with a genetic mother that never lived), the use of posthumous gametes (children from the grave) and even more simple issues, such as what to do with a long-standing DI patient whose husband has azoospermia, but who has walked out, yet the female patient wishes to continue with treatment.

Clearly the medical technology arising from the reproduction revolution, if not out of control, has moved on so quickly that it has left society and its morals behind (Lee, 1989; Strathern, 1992). As society and law try to catch up, there remain many potential loopholes and possibilities which urgently need examining and public debate (Van Dyck, 1995). In this chapter, I try to explore some of the issues and to outline some key areas where we must act as a matter of urgency. The issues of law, ethics and morals concerning ART could easily fill an entire book.

Morality

Common public morality is concerned with what the so-called average man in the street is at ease with. In terms of ART, the HFE Act of 1990 is supposed to reflect the public morality of the time, since laws are binding on everyone in society, irrespective of their own personal beliefs. It is also worth acknowledging here that there is also a difference between public and private morality. Within our frame of reference, this means that the public seems to accept the morality of providing access to ART for the infertile. However, what is not so clear is what public morality makes of issues concerning donor insemination (anonymous or known), surrogacy, sex selection, ovum donation for elderly post-menopausal women, the use of fetal tissue and embryo research, to name just a few of the debatable issues. According to the Warnock report (1984), key issues relating to what is morally acceptable as a bare minimum, are:

(1) Welfare of the child
(2) The integrity of the family unit
(3) Status of the prospective parents and those involved in helping them.

Public morality comes into the equation of male infertility mainly in the arena of donor insemination. Like surrogacy, advocates suggest that the morality of DI is a private matter of little concern to the public. Like homosexuality, provided it is done behind close doors, there is no need for public concern. Indeed, it is of interest to note that results from a number of surveys done in the 1980s suggest that DI is the least popular form of ART, in respect of public opinion. Nevertheless, provided the welfare of the child is not at stake, the 1990 Act allows for DI to be carried out, but only now in licensed clinics. Public morality also demonstrated increasing concerns about treatment during the late 1980s following on from the publication of the Warnock report in 1984.

The Human Fertilisation and Embryology Act 1990 and medical research

Prior to 1990, no Bill of the HFEA type had ever been placed before Parliament, representing a turning point in medical research. Members of Parliament argued that legislation was necessary to regulate research on human embryos. Furthermore, they claimed the integrity of reproductive medicine needed protection, whilst scientists and clinicians also needed protection from legal action or sanction. They also believed that people feared unregulated research, being uneasy about genetic interference to embryos (eugenics, human husbandry etc.).

Issues of concern and major controversies arising in the field of ART

Without doubt ART brings with it many philosophical, legal and moral questions. Other worries centre on the true costs of treatment, for example the cost of a live birth per treatment (varying between £12 000 to £25 000 depending on the unit), and the relative success of the treatment (IVF in 1993 produced an average live birth rate for all clinics of just 12%). The increasing incidence of multiple births was also a matter for grave concern. Issues over emotional costs were also considered to be vitally important.

Invariably, as societies develop, sometimes technology brings about possibilities which challenge mankind as a whole (Lee, 1989, 1992, 1993; Strathern, 1992; Van Dyck, 1995). Such issues include the use of donor semen, sex selection, surrogacy and in particular post-menopausal mothers. The field of ART in this way resembles a moral minefield. Public interest is immense, hence the weekly sensational headlines that inform us of the latest development. The reality of eugenics grows closer and closer. Public debate is intense and humanity must face some difficult decisions (Van Dyck, 1995). Men are involved in all these controversial treatment methods, although they do not necessarily specifically involve cases of male infertility.

Men's ideas and opinions on these issues need to be heard. How much do 60 and 70 year old men wish to be fathers of children born to post menopausal women old enough to be grandparents? Similar questions need to be asked about sex selection, surrogacy, etc. How do men feel about women having children without men by self insemination or DI? What does Virgin Birth Syndrome mean to men in the twentieth century? The ethics of providing DI treatment to single women outside of a stable relationship remain unclear. Individual clinics are left to their own devices regarding this particular conundrum (some might refer individual cases to their ethical committees, some will not refer the case, some will have an open policy and embrace the case, some will have a closed policy and refuse the case outright). Taken to extremes, it is possible to imagine a world where females rule the world and reproduction is achieved through insemination, using semen samples from donor banks.

Even in its short history, ART has already had its fair share of controversies. Septuplet pregnancies, embryo reduction, embryos for sale, Baby M, who should be offered or refused treatment, eggs for sale and so on. These have all been headline news during the past 15 years. Fertility techniques are now recognised for their most common side effect; that of multiple pregnancies. When it comes to IVF or GIFT, a substantial body of medical opinion insist that a flexible approach should be made in terms of the number of eggs or embryos transferred in any one treatment cycle. The HFEA put a ceiling of three on all treatment cycles. The majority of clinics are happy to comply, but throughout the world, in the UK, the USA, Australia, Singapore and a number of European countries, clinics have been happy to routinely transfer up to six eggs or embryos; in the belief that more means an improved chance of pregnancy. Yes, this may well be so, but the resulting side effects also produce large numbers of multiple pregnancies. There have been at least two well known IVF clinics in the world which to date have had their licences revoked for unethically transferring too many eggs or embryos. Whatever the merits of the arguments, statutory bodies throughout the world (currently in the UK, France and in Australia, others pending) insist that it is only ethical to transfer three eggs or embryos.

Here in the UK, Professor Ian Craft made history and newspaper headlines when he was allegedly interviewed by the police for his pioneering work with regard to embryo reduction. Many colleagues felt it was unethical to transfer more than three eggs or embryos and then to selectively kill off fetuses (embryo reduction involves imaging a fetus by ultrasound and then injecting potassium chloride or an embryotoxic drug directly into the fetal heart) *in utero* when high order multiple pregnancies resulted. At the very least the idea was described at one conference as being somewhat cavalier. Under the circumstances, Professor Craft was not indicted and as far as I am aware may still occasionally practise embryo reduction, when the fate of his patients is threatened by a high order multiple pregnancy, but the case certainly serves to highlight some of the controversies that may easily arise in this field.

The idea of embryos for sale is a little far fetched in the way that the press portrayed it when this controversy hit the front page. A clinic in the UK had allowed patients to take their own embryos away, and they subsequently ended up in a clinic in the USA. This generous and humanitarian act was castigated by the press. The HFEA were called in and there was a great deal of controversy. The case raised the issue of possible trafficking in gametes. This already happens to some extent with donor semen. Clinics happily sell semen from one clinic to another (so long as it is licensed). However, the idea of embryos being sold in a similar way for the use of recipients seems to horrify people. The issue was further exacerbated by the fact that the HFEA insists that gametes must be destroyed after five years in the freezer. So there was also the concern over wasted gametes, which is counterbalanced by the possibility that 'time warp' children, another of the oddities which Strathern suggests technology proliferates, might be created if this was not the case. Imagine two children conceived at the same time, but alive centuries apart (there are already up to fifty such siblings separated by up to ten years).

Other ethical worries centre on the posthumous use of gametes (children from the grave). In France, for instance, a legal ruling was made to allow one prospective mother to gain access to the stored semen of her recently deceased spouse, whilst in the USA, as far as I am aware, there have been a number of contrary rulings on access to stored embryos. This is a particularly emotive and difficult ethical issue. Are we to allow technology to throw up possibilities that deny nature (as some would put it)? Currently, in the UK, access to frozen gametes remains severely restricted and it is my belief that stored gametes of a deceased individual must and will be eventually destroyed. This issue will however, in my opinion, run on and on. We will yet see more high court rulings on this one.

The case of Baby M was definitely headline news in the USA. There, surrogacy in exchange for payment is legal, which is not the case in the UK (HF&E Act of 1990). This case centred on Baby M, who was kept by the surrogate mother, after she had promised to carry the child on behalf of and for the prospective adoptive mother and spouse of the baby's father. Here, in the UK, our most celebrated surrogate is Kim Cotton, who has successfully handed over babies twice now. Surrogacy is a legal minefield.

There have now been two celebrated cases involving patients contesting clinics' refusal to offer them treatment. One was in Manchester and the other in Sheffield, both in the UK. So far the score is one apiece, with the latest case going against the patient. The issue will continue to rumble on. Is it an undeniable right to reproduce? Is it different if treatment is on offer in the private sector or public sector? Does the morality of the patient(s) have a role in determining whether treatment should be offered or not? These remain difficult questions. Does a clinic have the right to tell a patient that they should call it a day? Is it right for another clinic to offer patients who have already had ten cycles of IVF, further treatment? The jury remains out on all these questions and I myself can find no easy answers.

The eggs for sale fiasco centred on a clinic that was offering free sterilisation to women willing to donate eggs to an ovum donation programme. Initially, the clinic was excoriated by the press and the HFEA was called in. Subsequently, the HFEA ruled that the clinic was acting ethically (although close to the dividing line) and press interest declined. These cases outline some of the existing ethical problems.

Consequences of the reproduction revolution

As technology moves on, we must begin to ask ourselves what are we doing with ART, and where it is taking us. The debate on the availability of ovary donation or on the use of fetal ovarian tissue also has wide-reaching repercussions. One of the greatest fears regarding fetal tissue use is that we will create children whose female biological parent will have never existed. Are we also about to embark on human husbandry (consider if this technology had been available to Hitler; he would have been able to ensure that all non-Aryan women became surrogates for Aryan babies. It might have provided a new type of final solution, which probably would also have appealed to certain extreme right wing white South Africans). What about the use of Caucasian donor semen or ova for coloured couples? Where do men stand with regard to all this?

Currently, other new possibilities under the microscope are ICSI, pre-implantation diagnosis and gene therapy.

What seems certain, is that as the reproduction revolution brings about so many new possibilities, that what previously was taken for granted in western society will not be so in the future (Strathern, 1992). Strathern observes that our kinship system is rapidly being distorted by the possibilities that reproduction technology brings about. The revolution that brings about reproduction without sex is setting off a chain reaction of events which are becoming and will become part of the crisis that mankind is facing as the millennium approaches, mainly because the possibilities presented by technology keep growing at a seemingly never ending and phenomenal rate. There is much useful material about the problems discussed in this section and the legal background in Morgan & Lee (1991).

Concerns with infertility and the need for regulation and legislation

As we can see technology brings new problems as well as new benefits. But there are also other costs. It is entirely possible that patients might be exploited by the purveyors of these new technologies, hence the urgent need for legislation in all countries where ART is practised. What is there currently to protect the innocent from abuse? In the UK and in Australia, laws are now in place. These laws seek to regulate practice and to provide some protection for patients. Unfortunately, in the USA, legislation is still not in place. It may be valuable to look at this area in greater detail.

With regard to patient abuse, the feminist lobby in particular has been most vociferous (Corea, 1985; Pfeffer & Woollett, 1983; Pfeffer, 1987; Scutt, 1990). One view of abuse is that high technology options are chosen in preference to the simpler methods; the so-called 'low tech' option. This idea receives support from some counsellors, sociologists and social workers and a number of people-related agencies. This seems to be an appropriate point to explore some of the issues. Scutt (1990) points out that many patients have unwittingly been used as guinea pigs. She feels that throughout the world and especially in the USA, many new clinics have started with very poor results. Her theme is that units have hidden their poor results from their unwitting patients. That progress has been achieved and financed by the ignorant who have queued for the 'high tech' treatments. There is some truth in the matter. Even as late as 1988 in USA, many IVF clinics, when surveyed had not yet achieved a live birth. Even the Jones Institute took a significant number of cases to produce the first delivery (as did Steptoe and Edwards in the UK).

Informed consent

Consideration of patient exploitation conveniently leads us to look at what constitutes informed consent. The HFEA certainly requires all clinics to obtain detailed and reasonable informed consent from patients. The importance of informed consent in the field of ART should not be underestimated. What then is informed consent within the context of this field? What is material information? Is omission of certain key information ethical or consistent with informed consent? In a field where average success rates are only 12% and by and large, sums of money in excess of £1000 are changing hands per treatment cycle, informed consent is vital. We must clearly consider a number of points: When patients are told the success rate, do they truly understand? Not necessarily so according to Scutt (1990) and others. Perhaps it is better to talk in terms of the average cost for a baby, or to point out that only one couple in ten will go home with a baby. Success rates are hard to understand properly, because they are presented in so many different ways. The only real meaningful data is the live birth rate per treatment cycle. Success rates per transfer or success rates including pregnancies which miscarry are not useful. Scutt (1990) further quotes Bates & Lapsley, who suggest that with advanced technology such as ART, where clinicians cannot agree, how can patients make truly informed consent. I concur with this statement. In my opinion, informed consent is a challenge for the field. Even now, with all the additional requirements imposed by the HFEA, I am of the opinion that few couples are giving truly informed consent to treatment. I would even go so far as to say that within the terms of the HFEA code of practice, we should be refusing treatment much more often on the basis that couples are not in a position to properly give their informed consent to treatment. The possibilities for litigation in the future could be immense, especially as patients become less enamoured with the field and those who work in it. Informed consent is our challenge for the 1990s.

Another way in which patients are disadvantaged is that finding a clinician is a haphazard process. If you find someone who insists on surgery, this is what you will get. Find a clinician with a physician's outlook and you may not have surgery. For instance, PCOD may be treated surgically by a gynaecologist, whereas an endocrinologist might choose a medical treatment with drugs. Knowing how to choose a specialist or clinic is a skill which might make a big difference to treatment outcome. The HFEA is currently exploring the idea of publishing a league table of clinic success rates. I am not necessarily sure this will help since one will rarely be comparing like with like, but it is a well meaning step in the right direction.

Funding for research

Looking at the ethics and morality of ART from a different perspective, it is worth considering the case of John Biggars, a senior experimental embryologist at Harvard University, who has been an adviser to the USA government. He has carried out extensive research into non-human primates. This work was recommended by the US government with a view to producing experimental data before pressing on with human treatment. As recently as 1988, Dr Biggars has been quoted as saying that if all governments had insisted on this approach, IVF might still be in suspension. The USA federal ethics board in 1979 considered IVF too experimental. Even today there is no NIH funding for IVF, a situation similar to that here in the UK (there is patchy government funding in the UK – Manchester, Hammersmith, Edinburgh and recently Newcastle).

Funding of other treatments such as IUI and GIFT is also haphazard here in the UK. In many ways, all ART, whether it be here in the UK, the USA, Australia or anywhere remains experimental. Whether we believe in this or not, we must question the ethics of continuing to allow ART to be practised whilst the definitive controlled prospective studies remain undone. Any area of medicine with such low success rates (most ART procedures produce live birth rates of no more than about 10% on average) would limit practice to specialised units until large studies proved the value of the work. Even kidney transplant surgery once yielded 10% success rates or less, but to have ART available on a widespread basis, when it is still relatively unproven is questionable ethically. Yet, because the patients want the treatment, ART has become acceptable.

Legislation

This seems a good point to look at legislation. Law is traditionally concerned with property. This is so in the UK, USA and Common-wealth countries. Ownership and proprietorship are key issues. Laws relating to people are only just becoming current. For example the legal status of DI children has only just been decided in a parental orders document in 1993 in the UK. As a consequence, DI children in the UK may now legally be recognised as the child of the 'adoptive' male parent without course to legal proceedings for adoption. In other words, at birth the 'adoptive' father may legally append his name to the birth certificate without the need to involve any lawyers. Nevertheless, legislation regarding human fertility and the provision of services therefore is sparse. Urgent legislation is needed to protect the interests of the patients.

History of legislation in the UK

In 1978 the first ever IVF baby was born in the UK. Even today there is no real NHS funding and little MRC funding. In 1984, the Warnock report was published and made sweeping recommendations. From 1984 till 1991, there was a voluntary licensing authority which carried out self-regulation. In 1991, following on from the HF&E Act of 1990, the HFEA became the recognised statutory body (laws in place). The HFEA has published and revised its code of practice and ensures that the code is strictly followed. The success of the HFEA in policing human reproduction in the UK remains to be seen. Already, a few clinics have been closed for various official reasons, but it remains to be seen whether the authority can ensure that certain routinely covert and questionable practices by clinics will be prevented.

Legislation in the USA

The regulation and policing of fertility treatments in the USA are closely related to the development of the Society for ART (SART) of the American Fertility Society (AFS). In 1981 the first USA IVF baby was born. As pointed out above (see paragraph concerning Professor John Biggars earlier in this chapter), there has never been any NIH funding, since IVF is considered and continues to be considered experimental and relatively unsuccessful. More proof of efficacy is required. By 1984, the AFS was already taking a lead in looking at the ethics of the field and considering the possibility of self regulation. The Society for ART was established circa 1987, and has provided national statistics from 1988 onwards. Standards and guidelines have been set through the AFS. There is still no clear current US policy, perhaps mainly because reproduction is viewed as a private and privileged matter, not to be interfered with by government. There is no prescribed uniform procedure for accurate recording of results nor disclosure of success rates. Nor is there any recognised means of certifying the professional competence of personnel.

The AFS has published the following articles and treatises

American Fertility Society (1986) Ethical considerations of the new reproductive technologies. *Fertil Steril*, **46** (Suppl 1).

American Fertility Society (1988) Ethical considerations of the new reproductive technologies. *Fertil Steril*, **49** (Suppl 1).

American Fertility Society (1990) Revised minimum standards for *in vitro* fertilization, gamete intrafallopian transfer, and related procedures. *Fertil Steril*, **53**, 225.

American Fertility Society (1990) New guidelines for the use of semen donor insemination. *Fertil Steril*, **53** (Suppl 1).

American Fertility Society (1990) Ethical considerations of the new reproductive technologies. *Fertil Steril*, **53** (Suppl 2).

Although there are no federal laws, five states have some laws, these are Kentucky, Illinois, Louisiana, New Mexico and Pennsylvania. Since 1975 there has been a moratorium on funding for embryo research. Even today most state governments remain uninterested in IVF. The provision of IVF is very diverse, ranging from university programmes to small private clinics. Professional qualifications are extremely disparate. There are current concerns over quality of services and claims of success rates. There is no federal support for patient fees, insurance cover is possible, which is not the case in the UK.

Legislation in Australia

In Australia, the first IVF baby was born in 1979. This was the first country to adopt legislation. The State of Victoria Infertility (Medical Procedures) Act 1984 ensured that patient's rights were enshrined in law. It was however unfortunately a tight and unpopular law. Patients resented the need for statutory counselling (there also exists a tremendous reluctance among patients in the UK to take up counselling). Clinics found regulations too draconian. In spite of the Infertility (Medical Procedures) (Amendments) Act 1987, research in Victoria has ground to a halt. The Reproductive Technology Act 1988 followed in South Australia. Currently other states still have not made any legislation. In both states with laws, IVF is limited to married couples only, and approximately half the cost of treatment is subsidised by the state.

Legislation concerning ART in the rest of the world

Legislation across the rest of the world is scarce. There now follows a brief resumé of the position in several other countries.

Canada: No legislation. No formal regulation or collection of data. Funding is essentially private. Society of Obstetrics and Gynaecology and Canadian Fertility Society have issued guidelines for practitioners. MRC of Canada has also published ethical guidelines.

France: First IVF baby 1981 (Jacque Testart and Rene Frydmann at Clamart). Most clinics belong to FIVNAT, which organises member clinics and collects data. Another major group is CECOS, which controls DI in France, but CECOS also carries out significant numbers of FIVET. Currently a National Commission regulates FIVET. Social security reimburses treatment. France is in process of introducing laws limiting research and banning ovum donation for elderly post menopausal women.

Italy: Here there is similar activity regarding ovum donation to France, particularly since Severino Antinori in Rome is a prime pioneer of the technique. No laws though are yet in place.

Germany: No regulatory body. Bill is in progress. Some reimbursement through insurance. Many private clinics. Proposed legislation is very strict. Little research takes place, and there is strict control over treatments. Clinical freedom is very limited. If proposed legislation is passed, all research will be banned. Even now, only limited number of ova inseminated, since all embryos must be transferred.

India: In 1994 legislation introduced to stop sex selection.

Singapore: Here government is looking at legislation, but as in Hong Kong no laws are yet in place.

Conclusion

The banner headlines that appear almost weekly in the national and world-wide press serve to highlight how the reproduction revolution has not only caught the public imagination but also how society is anxious and worried about some of its more sinister aspects, such as the potential use of fetal tissue. The field of assisted reproduction may be viewed as a moral and ethical minefield, because technology has outstripped the public understanding of what is on offer (Strathern, 1992; Van Dyck, 1995). As society struggles to come to terms with reproduction technology, some might argue for a moratorium on new advances, as exists currently in the USA, others might argue for carefully regulated research (as per the UK); whatever the case, public debate and public education regarding such matters is vital (Van Dyck, 1995). Government legislation and regulatory bodies such as we have here in the UK are natural ways of addressing the issues of ethics and morals of assisted reproduction, but in my opinion, this is just a start. The HFEA is to be congratulated on its stance over recent controversies such as sex selection and donated ovarian tissue, however, more needs to be done urgently.

Mankind as a whole must also take collective responsibility. If our expectations have changed in a world that is also changing rapidly, we must ensure that our desires are balanced by an adult outlook rather than one clouded by infantile wants (Strathern, 1992). The field of ART must resist the attitude that science must provide a child at any cost. It is not without reason that the HFEA code of practice makes the unusual, but necessary, issue over the welfare of the child (unconceived and unborn).

Consideration of the potential of abuse of the technology is also important. In a field which is largely devoid of public funding (particularly in the UK and USA) the potential for patient exploitation is obvious. With this in mind, the issue of informed consent becomes a key consideration. It is vital that every clinic ensures that its patients are able to make a choice of prospective treatment in a manner both free from pressure (coercion) and from ignorance.

Even now, too many countries lack legislation, funding for research and treatment, which means that many people in the world are potentially open to abuse because of the absence of regulation and insufficient public debate and education. Mankind urgently needs to catch up with the shirt tails of the reproduction revolution. The appearance of male infertility on the agenda of the major arena is just one aspect of this ongoing scenario.

Chapter 12
Discussion and Conclusion

Summary

Counselling in infertility is a highly specialised area. I hope it has become equally clear that counselling in male infertility is also a sub-specialism. So much so that a large part of this book has been necessarily highly technical, but as I have already mentioned before, the lack of this technical knowledge will serve only as a hindrance when dealing with male infertility clients. I hope that the chapters on both diagnosis and the treatment of male infertility will give anyone (counsellor, gynaecologist, urologist, embryologist, nurse, etc.) reading this book, sufficient information on how infertility specialists manage their male patients.

In Chapter 4, I have introduced the idea of guilt and how this leads both men and women into isolation. Because women feel the same emotions (albeit for slightly different reasons) I have chosen to deal with how men specifically deal and come to terms with male infertility in separate chapters (in Chapters 5 and 6). I am particularly stricken at how Hite's (1991) depiction of male ideology fits in so well with the themes and hypotheses in this book (and role models on ideology; see also Chapter 7, on the effects of childhood development on how men respond) regarding men's responses to infertility. It is remarkable that in both sexes, the issue of punishment is also a common theme. This idea of punishment then seems to go hand in hand with the idea of crime and punishment; in other words, to be punished as they are with child-lessness, they reason that they must have committed a grievous crime, which leads to their need for forgiveness. Hence, as I point out in Chapter 1, Man in Crisis, some couples appear to feel a need to pay for their treatment as a modern way of atonement, which then paves the way to conception.

In Chapter 5, I have explored men's responses to a diagnosis of male infertility. Men are victims of their own male ideology. Men must cope, runs the orthodoxy and so they do not need nor seek the help of others (Lee, 1995a). Indeed men hurt men terribly. Those that have children or those who have not had a diagnosis of male infertility, seem only capable of mockery. They offer their 'stricken' colleagues cruelty rather than succour (Lee, 1995a; Mason, 1993). The reaction of colleagues and male friends therefore serves to reinforce the isolation, low self esteem and pain of those diagnosed as having male infertility. Thus many such men become depressed, some may be angry, many will face crisis as their beliefs (about life in general, about their own expectations of being a father) have been challenged almost to breaking point by the diagnosis. Indeed for those who feel that their manhood has been called into question, episodes of impotence will arise. In the same chapter, male ambivalence about fatherhood is also explored, which also makes the idea of acceptance of childlessness as an equally important consideration as the pursuit of treatment itself. It is also important to consider the possibility that success, becoming a father, may also be equally threatening to a man. The fact that many men walk out on their families (Strathern, 1993) adds weight to the argument.

Interestingly, as male ideology is explored, the almost unique source of support for men diagnosed as infertile is their wives and/or female partners (Mason, 1993). Is this a paradoxical fulfilment of male ideology or women rising above the pettiness of their subjugation or are they remaining true to their female ideology? Perhaps the answer lies in all three possibilities.

I am in no doubt that male infertility dovetails very neatly with Greenstein's idea that man in general (not necessarily mankind) is in a state of crisis. The changing role of women has undoubtedly contributed to man's decline (Greenstein, 1993). As women become more assertive, as they assume more power, go out to work, become more independent (especially regarding their own spending power), they are losing their traditional reliance on men as husbands (and the system of male ideology) and are therefore rapidly redressing the balance (Greenstein, 1993). This, as well as the erosion of Western man's systems of roles, rituals, symbols and taboos (Bee & Mitchell, 1982; Levinson, 1978), has effectively placed both man and mankind (including women) in a state of crisis. Although the problem is clearly a collective one, I have in the main dwelt on how this crisis has affected men.

In some ways, in spite of overwhelming evidence that environmental factors also play a large role (*The Lancet*, editorial, 1995), it almost looks as if the crisis may be contributing to male infertility, as well as being a side effect of it. This idea needs further investigation. Nevertheless, it seems to me that man in crisis and many couples' feelings of punishment (being punished for some unknown, but probably heinous crime), which are driven by guilt (Lee, 1995a), colludes to bring about a new Messianic age where the old gods of fertility have effectively returned (albeit in a new form; as Strathern (1992) has said, when old images are reproduced, the reproduction is never exact) with those who provide treatment being in the new guise of high priests and priestesses in their new temples (infertility clinics). It is also important to remember that the pursuit of fertility is all about having children, which is how we reproduce ourselves, which, no matter which culture or society you belong to, seems to be a vital fact of life (MacCormack & Strathern (eds.), 1980). As roles and rituals have been eroded, one of Western peoples' last great symbols of life is the child. Children are a symbol of hope, indeed so strong a symbol that children now dominate the news media. Effectively, we not only have a reborn fertility cult in the West, but also a cult of children, which has been a vital cog in the re-emergence of fertility as a modern cult.

Since so many of my hypotheses hinge on the idea of male ideology, this concept is explored in Chapter 7. It seems all pervasive in the Western world and would appear to be imprinted during childhood development through role modelling (Bee & Mitchell, 1982; Crawshaw, 1995; Hite, 1991). Infertility in general, as well as the arena of male infertility, has much to teach us about adapting to a new, more equal, type of person ideology (Van Hoose & Worth, 1982). The way in which men are reduced to powerless pawns (sperm providers) in infertility clinics serves as a powerful impetus to think and look differently at the world. Peter Humm's (1989) outlook on his own experience reveals tremendous insight on how men might change their outlooks. It is possible that in the microcosm of male infertility, we have an allegory of the global situation of man in crisis. As one mirrors the other, possibly the way men cope with infertility in the future will help them also adapt to the problems they face with respect to Greenstein's (1993) view of man coping with a new world order.

Much of the book is dominated by Western opinions and outlook. In Chapter 8 the influences of the aforementioned factors are examined. For example, vast numbers of people in the world belong to religions which control their reproductive rights and options, whilst many people have experiences of both Western and non-Western medical systems, all of which different people from different cultures will swear by. In the process of the exploration, it was remarkable how all pervasive the issue of fertility is. It seems to dominate religions; 'go forth and multiply' being a basic message to believers of most religions; just as the ideas of the cyclical nature of life and rebirth also dominate religions (and the depths of peoples' psyche). When dealing with male infertility, if this chapter (albeit brief and far from comprehensive) serves to remind the practitioner to keep in mind the patient's/client's religious, ethnic and cultural background, it will have done its job.

Donor insemination is dealt with in passing in Chapter 3, and in greater detail in Chapter 9. Here, some historical background is given as well as some information on the regulation of DI and how it is organised. The social and psychological aspects of DI are considered with a section on the implications of taking up DI treatment. Male infertility and DI do not necessarily go hand in hand (Lee, 1995a; Mason, 1993), but where a couple are able to make an informed decision to proceed without prejudicing the future survival of their relationship, it is a means to an end.

The history of women in medicine and particularly the dominance of men in gynaecology (Chapter 10) makes for interesting reading (Finkelstein, 1989; Jordanova, 1980). Furthermore, it seems to explain, in part, the dearth of interest in male infertility, at a time when reproduction as a whole is undergoing revolutionary changes. The impact of male ideology is not lost here either, serving to reinforce a medical agenda that has dominated for centuries. Feminist outrage at this medical agenda portrays a significant viewpoint (Corea, 1985; Pfeffer, 1987; Scutt, 1990). The future way of addressing this agenda must lie in more women coming into the discipline of obstetrics and gynaecology and in them making it into the higher grade jobs. Until then, we must rely on men being more able to ask for help and in male specialists being more willing to accept that when it comes to infertility, the female is not the only part of the equation.

In counselling men (Chapter 6) it is assumed that the reader has read most of the foregoing chapters, particularly Chapters 4 and 5; indeed a quick delve into Chapter 7 is also warranted. In Chapter 6, the male response to diagnosis of infertility is summarised after which a model is proposed, and is illustrated by an idealised composite case history.

Although this is a book concerned with male infertility, the ramifications of moral and ethical issues relating to the whole field of infertility are relevant. I make no apologies therefore for the wider discussions aired in the chapter on the legal, ethical and moral aspects of assisted reproduction technology. In Chapter 11 issues of concern are examined and considerable space is given over to some real life case histories which have confronted those working in the field. Public morality is discussed along with the need to allay public fears and concerns (a matter discussed in Van Dyck, 1995). In some countries, such concerns have led to legislation, which is also given considerable attention. Unfortunately, there is still insufficient regulation of ART throughout the world and the reproduction revolution continues to leave public understanding and consensus in its wake (Lee, 1993; Strathern, 1992; Van Dyck, 1995). Issues such as fetal tissue donation, sex selection and eugenics continue to arouse public concern, which is unlikely to abate, until these issues have received adequate public debate (Lee, 1993; Van Dyck, 1995). Until such time these controversial issues will continue or not according to gut reactions rather than through reason and a true understanding of the real issues (Strathern, 1992).

This chapter cannot be closed without a detailed consideration of a new treatment option for male infertility (outlined in Chapter 3). In spite of the impact of ICSI (even now, at the time of writing, after 18 months, fewer than 2000 babies have been born from ICSI world-wide) male infertility has yet to come out into the open in a significant way. The danger of becoming carried away with ICSI is that whilst ICSI benefits, all the other avenues which have only just come to the fore will again be left in the doldrums. In particular, here we are talking about diagnostic methods (we still need urgently to define a global method of assessing sperm function; who for instance will benefit best from ICSI?) and improved understanding of male fertility. Furthermore, even if the best units are able to maintain 25% delivery rates, more patients will still fail than succeed. Moreover, ICSI is likely to suffer the same problems that GIFT had, in other words regression towards the mean.

Inevitably, as more and more units offer ICSI, results are likely to become more and more pedestrian. Consider IVF. This is a treatment option which has not changed much in delivery rates from 1985 till now 1995. National data indicates IVF remaining as a 10% procedure (HFEA annual reports for 1993 and 1994). Do some units get better results? Do those units that get better results select patients more carefully? Are all units reporting results in the same way? Assuming these minor details are adjusted for and we accept that some units really are achieving 25%, we might assume that these units have the best expertise, well equipped laboratories and theatres, sufficient capital backing to maintain standards and sufficient patient throughput to ensure that experience levels are also maintained. In my experience, units able to manage the above will remain reasonably successful. However, because successful IVF may be likened to the pursuit of excellence and perfection, continual loss of staff represents loss of considerable experience and expertise.

I mentioned earlier that the growth in IVF units in just the past ten years has been phenomenal (from 10 to more than 100). One question comes quickly to mind. As training in IVF is a 12–24 month affair, where have all these so-called trained personnel come from? As more and more trained personnel emerge from existing units, who is replacing them? One answer is that the established larger clinics bear a burden of constantly training new personnel, who are quite likely to leave as soon as they are trained. There is a high turnover of staff in the IVF world. Inevitably, in my opinion, something has to give in these situations. The above describes one reason why IVF currently remains a 10% procedure. If we accept the above scenario and we accept that ICSI requires even more expertise (not every embryologist will be capable of excellent micromanipulation) then, if we see ICSI offered by every unit, we may see ICSI rapidly become a 5% procedure. I urge caution on two fronts therefore, first because ICSI may end up being a transient phenomenon and secondly because if we invest all our energies in ICSI, we undo a lot of good work that had begun to bear fruit with regard to research on male infertility.

Many things remain unchanged though. At the time of writing, infertility is beginning to be recognised as a specialist subject by the Royal College of Obstetrics and Gynaecology and there are now several formally trained consultants in reproductive medicine. However, the sub-specialist subject of male infertility still relies on a person's individual interest and willingness to research the subject. There is still no globally recognised test of sperm function, but researchers such as John Aitken, Harry Moore and Chris Barrett (in the UK) continue to work towards this goal.

Apart from ICSI, which as I mentioned earlier runs the risk of being used as a global panacea for male infertility, where there are surgically correctable problems, surgery may be considered, but even this produces variable results. If there are clear endocrinological problems, drug therapy may be useful. In the main, 60–70% of all male infertility is of unexplained aetiology. Perhaps one half of this group will have to seriously consider ICSI, but the cost is high both in monetary and emotional terms. The other half may consider IUI, GIFT, traditional IVF (ICSI still needs IVF) and other options, but at the end of the day, no-one has yet proven any of these treatments to be appropriate in cases of male infertility; the definitive controlled studies have still not been done and the jury is still out on this matter.

It is not hard to imagine the pull of ICSI, when there are few possible other options. This, in addition to the shock and crisis that diagnosis brings, means that the general hopelessness of the situation is almost too much to bear. Men therefore suffer from two serious responses, total denial (a way of survival) and isolation (Lee, 1995a; Mason, 1993; Monach, 1993). I have explored superficially the idea of how male ideology traps men into denial and isolation. Male supremacy has meant that men are not supposed to need help nor to seek it. Men must endure or be deemed to be weak. It is a *Catch 22* situation. Men respond and cope with male infertility in a variety of ways. They also seek a variety of different treatments. Some will accept DI as a means to an end, but unlike women (many of whom readily accept donor eggs) men find it a difficult issue to deal with.

Because of men's response to male infertility, working with men on an individual basis can be a difficult and slow process. People in general may be resistant to the idea of counselling, but men, in particular those with male infertility, are on the widest edge of the spectrum (Lee, 1995a; Mason, 1993; Monach, 1993). I have outlined a model and looked at ways in which men might be facilitated to move on. The methods are by no means cast iron guaranteed (there are too many variations in the human mind and spirit to allow us even to generalise remotely), but I hope that some principles are set down and may be useful as a guideline in finding the way in when others are confronted with such clients.

Conclusion

This book is not intended to be a weighty definitive tome on male infertility. If I had set out with this objective in mind, the book has failed to achieve it. What I hope to have done is to provide the skeleton on to which much flesh needs to be added. Perhaps I have begun also to signpost the areas which we need to explore and understand when dealing with men who are infertile, and the diagnosis of which seems to strike at the very core of their existence.

On the assumption that ICSI is not a panacea for male infertility and bearing in mind, some men seem to have a strong desire to know why they have been unlucky enough to be subfertile or infertile, we still have a long way to go before we understand all we need to about male fertility. I hope it has become clear throughout the book that part of the mystery of male infertility lies in our ignorance. We do not yet know what constitutes a good sperm or a bad one. We have yet to determine why so many sperm? Nor do we know whether any sperm, moving or otherwise will do (many times have I heard it said, 'it only takes one'). Indeed, even in our schools, human reproduction is a taboo subject, which cannot be mentioned without sniggering and tittering. Perhaps fundamental changes in education itself and in the way men are brought up are needed before male infertility can be discussed openly and maturely.

As I have mentioned in Chapters 1, 7 and 8 male ideology has contributed greatly to the way in which men respond to a diagnosis of male infertility. To date, over several millennia, women have been subjugated as a consequence of the dominance of men throughout the world. In the West, the balance is beginning to redress itself. Women are becoming more assertive and taking control of their own lives, perhaps in some ways the reproduction revolution is a further manifestation of this (except that the feminists would take issue with this). Nevertheless, male role models remain the same for the time being. However, just as women are able to break free from their own subordinate ideology, there is hope for men, but it will mean major adjustments, whereby men might benefit from developing the emotional side of their characters and to be freer in how they express their emotions. When the time comes that men and women are able to share equally in life, much of the stigma over male infertility (and infertility in general) will disappear and furthermore, the world may indeed be a better place to live in.

Ignorance alone, however, is insufficient to explain all the problems that exist in the field. The lack of formal training in the discipline needs to be corrected, but this would seem to be a long-term project rather than one which will be attended to within the next five years. Once there is formal training available, standards will become tighter and there should be a lot less freedom of expression, meaning essentially that differences of opinion will disappear as more global standards will be established. These standards will arise because more research will be done, leaving less openings for opinions based purely on subjective observations (what is perceived rather than what is real). Most experts will consequently agree on more issues than they disagree, as is currently the case. Once a discipline becomes formalised, there is more opportunity for it to expand, as most specialists shy away from esoteric fields. Formal training will perhaps bring reproduction into the medical mainstream. This should both serve to improve treatments as well as make them more widely available.

We must not forget that the non-Western world also has much to teach us about male infertility. The way different cultures deal with the problem is particularly instructive. Not only are cross-cultural perspectives of value, but we must also keep in mind the value of religious and ethnic outlooks on issues of both fertility and sociopsychology. To ignore these issues would be like ignoring the collective knowledge of mankind as a whole.

How a man feels when he realises that becoming a parent, a father, might not be so easy as he originally thought, clearly relates to his outlook as a man. Because we all have role models which we follow, and because male ideology produces supposedly self reliant and self contained individuals, most men suffer terribly when told that they are infertile. How we begin to deal with men who feel the blow so badly is one part of the mystery. Where individuals are resistant to asking for or receiving help, the impotent render those who would help impotent. I have tried to signpost how we might begin attending to such clients. At the end of the day, I am also convinced that part of the key also lies in becoming adept at the art of counselling without counselling (now there's a thought). One way forward is to try to understand men better. By having discussed the issue of why men wish to be fathers and examining a few aspects of male childhood development, we are just beginning to open up areas about which we urgently need more information. As we learn more about these areas and as we can begin to reduce the stigma of male infertility, we may be able to achieve better intervention through counselling and certainly through the use of counselling skills within the infertility setting.

Looking to the future, I think it is clear in the book that I believe mankind is on the threshold of great social changes, particularly in the West but not just here. Life has become more and more disordered, family life is almost rendered asunder and the reproduction revolution has progressed so quickly that it has outstripped our moral and ethical boundaries; we are looking into the maelstrom. However, things may not be as bleak as I paint. Part of this change involves sharing more with our female partners – man must adapt to his environment. There is a new order (a new sheriff has come to town) where the male ideology that has dominated for the past 1500 years must give way to something new. We may certainly reject feminist ideology, but somewhere in between lies a fairer and better ideology which will create a better society, which will be able to utilise the benefits of our reproduction revolution in a better way. The revolution we are talking about is a form of *reproduction without sex*, which is ironic, since the decade before IVF arrived was the beginning of the era of *sex without reproduction* (both the sexual revolution and the pill). Thus, out of the crisis, will emerge a new order, where the gift of procreation will be seen in a clearer light. It is to be hoped that included in the new order will be a better way of dealing with men and male infertility. Nevertheless, the cult of children which has fuelled the re-emergence of a fertility cult whose new temples are the infertility clinics, where patients come to redeem (payment as atonement) themselves in order to achieve conception, seems to be with us for now and the foreseeable future.

Bibliography and References

Adcock, C.J. (1976) *Fundamentals of psychology*. Penguin, Harmondsworth.

American Fertility Society (1986) Ethical considerations of the new reproductive technologies. *Fertil Steril*, **46** (Suppl 1).

American Fertility Society (1988) Ethical considerations of the new reproductive technologies. *Fertil Steril*, **49** (Suppl 1).

American Fertility Society (1990) Revised minimum standards for *in vitro* fertilization, gamete intrafallopian transfer, and related procedures. *Fertil Steril*, **53**, 225.

American Fertility Society (1990) New guidelines for the use of semen donor insemination. *Fertil Steril*, **53** (Suppl 1).

American Fertility Society (1990) Ethical considerations of the new reproductive technologies. *Fertil Steril*, **53** (Suppl 2).

Anon (1994) Counselling in male infertility. Reproduced from *Working with Men*, in *Issue* (summer), p.6.

d'Ardenne, P. & Mahtani, A. (1989) *Transcultural Counselling in Action*. Sage, London.

Atkinson, D.R., Morten, G. & Sue, D.W. (1985) *Counselling American Minorities: A cross-cultural perspective*, 2nd ed. W.C. Brown, Dubuque, U.S.A.

Ayalon, O. (1990) *Crisis and Coping with Suicide and Bereavement*. Nord Publications, Haifa.

Bee, H.L. & Mitchell, S.K. (1984) *The Developing Person: A Lifespan Approach*, 2nd ed. Harper and Row, New York.

Berg, B.J., Wilson, J.F. & Weingartner, P.J. (1991) Psychological sequelae of infertility treatment: the role of gender and sex-role identification. *Soc Sci Med*, **33**, 1071–1080.

Bernt, H., Bernt, W.D. & Tacke, S. (1992) Sterilitat-Frauensache? Bewaltigungsverhalten und Paarstruktur von sterilen Paaren verschiedener Diagnosegruppen. *Psychother Psychosom Med Psychol*, **42**, 236–41.

Bloch, M. & Bloch, J. (1980) Women and the dialectics of nature in eighteenth-century French thought. In: *Nature, Culture and Gender* (eds C. MacCormack & M. Strathern), pp.25–41. Cambridge University Press, Cambridge.

Bor, R. & Scher, I. (1995) A family-systems approach to infertility counselling. In *Infertility Counselling* (ed. S. Jennings), pp.94–112. Blackwell Science Ltd, Oxford.

Bromham, D.R., Balmer, B., Clay, R. & Hamer, R. (1988) Disenchantment with infertility services: a survey of patients in Yorkshire. *British Journal of Family Planning*, **14**, 3–8.

Bromwich, P., Cohen, J., Stewart, I. & Walker, A. (1994) Decline in sperm counts: an artefact of changed reference range of 'normal'? *British Medical Journal*, **309**, 19–22.

Bronson, R.A., Fus, F., Cooper, G.W. & Phillips, D.M. (1990) Antisperm antibodies induce polyspermy by promoting adherence of human sperm to zonal-free hamster eggs. *Human Reproduction*, **5**, 690–696.

Brown, R. (1994) Big boys don't cry. *Issue* (Summer), pp.3–4.

Butt, W.R. (1982) *Human Reproductive Hormones*. Amersham International PLC, Amersham.

Cabau, A. & de Senarclens, M. (1986) Psychological aspects of infertility. In: *Infertility: Male and Female* (eds. V. Insler & B. Lunenfeld), pp. 648–72. Churchill Livingstone, New York.

Campbell, J. (1995) The fertile ground: the role of art therapy in the fertility clinic. In: *Infertility Counselling* (ed. S. Jennings), pp.113–132. Blackwell Science Ltd, Oxford.

Carlsen, B., Giwereman, A., Keiding, N. & Skakkebaek, N.E. (1992) Evidence for decreasing quality of semen during the past 50 years. *British Medical Journal*, **305**, 609–613.

Connolly, K.J., Edelmann, R.J., Cooke, I.D. & Robson, J. (1992) The impact of infertility on psychological functioning. *Journal of Psychosomatic Research*, **36**, 459–468.

Corea, G. (1985) *The Mother Machine*. Harper and Row (New York); The Women's Press, London.

Craft, I., Lee, S. & Ah-Moye, M. (1987) Gamete intra-fallopian transfer: the human experience. Proceedings of the Society for the Study of Fertility. J Reprod Fert, **80**, 663–672.

Crawshaw, M. (1995) Offering woman-centred counselling in reproductive medicine. In *Infertility Counselling* (ed S. Jennings), pp. 38–65. Blackwell Science Ltd, Oxford.

Davies, W.A.R., Dhariwal, H.S. & Lee, S. (1988) GIFT and IUI in the district general hospital. *Human Reproduction*, **3**, 611–612.

Editorial (1995) Male reproductive health and environmental oestrogens. *The Lancet*, **345**, 933–935.

Egan, G. (1990) *The Skilled Helper*, 4th ed. Brookes/Cole, California.

Erian, J. & Lee, S. (1990) Bovine mucus penetration as a test of sperm function. *J Reprod Fert*, Abstract Series No. 5, 69.

Farrow, S. (1994) Falling sperm quality, fact or fiction. *British Medical Journal*, **309**, 1–2.

Finkelstein, J. (1990) Women, pregnancy and childbirth. In *The Baby Machine* (ed. J.A. Scutt), pp.12–32. Green Print, London.

Gillan, P. (1987) *Sex Therapy Manual*. Blackwell Science Ltd, Oxford.

Gillison, G. (1980) Images of nature in Gimi thought. In *Nature, Culture and Gender* (eds. C. MacCormack & M. Strathern), pp.143–173. Cambridge University Press, Cambridge.

Ginsberg, J., Okolo, S., Prelevic, G. & Hardiman, P. (1994) Residence in London area and sperm density. *The Lancet*, **343**, 230.

Glover, T.D., Barrett, C.L.R., Tyler, J.P.P. & Hennessey, J.F. (1990) *Human Male Fertility and Semen Analysis*. Academic Press, London.

Goodale, J.C. (1980) Gender, sexuality and marriage: a Kaulong model of nature and culture. In *Nature, Culture and Gender* (eds. C. MacCormack and M. Strathern), pp.119–142. Cambridge University Press, Cambridge.

Greenstein, B. (1993) *The Fragile Man.* Boxtree, London.

Greer, G. (1991) *The Female Eunuch.* Flamingo, Glasgow.

Hall, L.A. (1991) *Male Sexuality 1900–1950.* Polity Press, Cambridge.

Harrison, R.F. (1986) Psychosocial aspects of infertility. *Irish Journal of Medical Science,* **155** (Suppl), 5–8.

Heggenhougen, H.K. (1980) Fathers and childbirth: an anthropological perspective. *Journal of Nurse Midwifery,* **25**, 21–26.

Henderson, B.B., Benton, B. & Cosgrove, M. *et al.* (1976) Urogenital tract abnormalities in sons of women treated with diethylstibestrol. *Paediatrics,* **58**, 505–507.

Hite, S. (1991) *The Hite Report on Love, Passion and Emotional Violence.* MacDonald Optima, London.

Hull, M. (1991) Infertility treatment: needs & effectiveness. Report published by the University of Bristol.

Humm, P. (1989) Waiting for a child. In: *Infertility/Women Speak Out* (ed. R.D. Klein), pp.51–58. Pandora Press (London).

Irvine, D.S. (1992) Assessment of spermatogenesis. *Current Obstetrics and Gynaecology,* **2**, 20–26.

Irvine, D.S. (1994) Falling sperm quality. *British Medical Journal,* **309**, 476.

Jakobovits, I. (1990) The status of the embryo in the Jewish tradition. In *The Status of the Human Embryo: Perspectives from Moral Tradition* (eds. G.R. Dunstan & M.J. Sellers), pp.62–73. King Edward's Hospital Fund for London.

Janosik, E.H. (ed.) (1984) *Crisis Counselling: A Contemporary Approach.* Wentworth, Belmont CA.

Jennings, S. (1988) Rights and rites? Innovation in the teaching of medical students at the London Hospital. *Holistic Medicine,* **3**, 185–194.

Jennings, S. (1995) Birthmasks: Ritualization and metaphor in fertility counselling. In *Infertility Counselling* (ed. S. Jennings), pp.133–150. Blackwell Science Ltd, Oxford.

Jennings, S. & Lee, S. (1995) Infertility counselling and medical diagnosis. In *Infertility Counselling* (ed. S. Jennings), pp.13–21. Blackwell Science Ltd, Oxford.

Jequier, A. (1986) *Infertility in the Male.* Churchill Livingstone, Edinburgh.

Jequier, A. & Crich, J. (1986) *Semen Analysis: A Practical Guide.* Blackwell Science Ltd, Oxford.

Jordanova, I.J. (1980) Natural facts: a historical perspective on science and sexuality. In *Nature, Culture and Gender* (eds. C. MacCormack & M. Strathern), pp.42–69. Cambridge University Press, Cambridge.

Kemeter, P. (1990) Studies on psychosomatic implications of infertility: Effects of emotional stress on fertilization and implantation in *in-vitro* fertilization. *Human Reproduction,* **3**, 341.

Klock, S.C. & Maier, D. (1992) Psychological factors related to donor insemination. *Fertil Steril,* **56**, 489–495.

Koval, R. & Scutt, J.A. (1990) Genetic and reproductive engineering – all for the infertile? In *The Baby Machine* (ed. J.A. Scutt), pp.33–57. Green Print, London.

Kutner, N.G. & Brogan, D. (1990) Gender roles, medical practice roles and ob-gyn career choice: a longitudinal study. *Women Health*, **16**, 99–117.

Lee, S., Craft, I., Brinsden, P. *et al.* (1987) Preliminary results from the Humana IVF program. Proceedings of the Society for the Study of Fertility. *Journal of Reproduction and Fertility*, **80**, 663–672.

Lee, S. (1988a) Intrauterine insemination. *Conceive*, **11**, 6–7.

Lee, S. (1988b) Sperm preparation for assisted conception. *Conceive*, **12**, 4–5.

Lee, S. (1989) The dilemma of the reproduction revolution. *Journal of the Royal Society of Health*, **109**, 10–11.

Lee, S. (1990) Is the presence of sperm autoimmunity in males meaningful? *Journal of Reprod and Fert*, Abstract Series No. **5**, 11.

Lee, S. (1991a) Biologists' involvement in the reproduction revolution. *Biologist*, **38**, 85–88.

Lee, S. (1991b) *Andrology*. BUPA Hospital Press, Leicester.

Lee, S. (1991c) *What it means to be a sperm trooper*. BUPA Hospital Press, Leicester.

Lee, S. (1992) Dilemmas of replacing sex with science. Letters. *Evening Standard*.

Lee, S. (1993) Choice of a baby's sex. *The Lancet*, **341**, 762.

Lee, S. & Mascarenhas, L. (1993) The NHS and the provision of fertility services. *Med-Tech*, **24**, 20.

Lee, S. (1994a) Male infertility. *The Lancet*, **344**, 415.

Lee, S. (1994b) Counselling in the infertility setting. *Journal of Fertility Counselling*, **1**, 21–25.

Lee, S. (1994c) Everything you wanted to know about semen analysis, but were afraid to ask. *MLW*, May, 9–10.

Lee, S. (1995a) Factors in male infertility. In *Infertility Counselling* (ed. S. Jennings), pp.66–78. Blackwell Science Ltd, Oxford.

Lee, S. (1995b) Appendix 1. Medical acronyms and important word glossary. In *Infertility Counselling* (ed. S. Jennings), pp.253–259. Blackwell Science Ltd, Oxford.

Lee, S. (1995c) Appendix 2. Treatment options for the infertile. In *Infertility Counselling* (ed. S. Jennings), pp.260–263. Blackwell Science Ltd, Oxford.

Levinson, D.J. (1978) *The Seasons of Man's Life*. Knopf, New York.

Maccoby, E. & Jacklin, C. (1974) *The Psychology of Sex Differences*. Stanford University Press, Stanford.

MacCormack, C.P. (1980a) Nature, culture and gender: a critique. In *Nature, Culture and Gender* (eds. C. MacCormack & M. Strathern), pp.1–24. Cambridge University Press, Cambridge.

MacCormack, C.P. (1980b) Proto-social to adult: a Sherbro transformation. In *Nature, Culture and Gender* (eds. C. MacCormack & M. Strathern), pp.95–118. Cambridge University Press, Cambridge.

MacCormack, C. & Strathern, M. (eds.) (1980) *Nature, Culture and Gender*. Cambridge University Press, Cambridge.

Mahlstedt, P.P. (1985) The psychological component of infertility. *Fertil Steril*, **43**, 335–346.

Mascarenhas, L., Khastgir, G., Davies, W.A.R. & Lee, S. (1994) Superovulation and timed intercourse: can it provide a reasonable alternative for those unable to afford assisted conception? *Human Reproduction*, **9**, 67–70.

Mason, M.C. (1993) *Male Infertility – Men Talking*. Routledge, London.

Masters, W.H., Johnson, V.E. & Kolodny, R.C. (1982) *Masters and Johnson on Sex and Human Loving*. Papermac, London.

Mead, M. (1996) *Male and Female*. W. Morrow, New York.

Menning, B.E. (1980) The emotional needs of infertile couples. *Fertil Steril*, **34**, 313–319.

Metheny, W.P., Blount, H. & Holzman, H. (1991) Considering obstetrics and gynaecology as a speciality: current attractors and detractors. *Obstet Gynecol*, **78**, 308–312.

Ministry of Environment and Energy, Denmark (1995) *Male Reproductive Health and Environmental Chemicals with Estrogenic Effect*. Miljoprojekt nr 290 1995. Danish Environmental Protection Agency, Copenhagen.

Monach, J.H. (1993) *Childless: No Choice. The Experience of Involuntary Childlessness*. Routledge, London.

Morgan, D. & Lee, R.G. (1991) *A Guide to the Human Fertilisation & Embryology Act 1990: Abortion & Embryo Research, the New Law*. Blackstone Press Ltd, London.

Odent, M. (1994) *Birth Reborn*. Souvenir Press, London.

O'Moore, A.M. (1986) Counselling and support systems for infertile couples. *Irish Journal of Medical Science*, **155** (Suppl), 12–16.

Oldereid, N.B., Rui, H. & Purvis, K. (1991) Menn under infertilitetsutredning. *Tidask Nor Laegeforen*, **111**, 1265–1268.

Ortner, S.B. (1974) Is female to male as nature is to culture. In *The anthropologist as hero* (eds. E.N. Hayes & T. Hayes), pp.70–107. MIT Press, Cambridge, Mass.

Owens, D.J., Edelman, R.E. & Humphrey, M.E. (1993) Male infertility and donor insemination: couples decisions, reactions and counselling needs. *Human Reproduction*, **8**, 880–885.

Palti, Z. (1969) Psychogenic male infertility. *Psychosom Med*, **31**, 326–330.

Parry, G. (1990) *Coping with Crises*. Routledge, London.

Pfeffer, N. (1987) Artificial insemination, in-vitro fertilization and the stigma of infertility. In *Reproductive Technologies* (ed. M. Stanworth). Polity Press, Oxford.

Pfeffer, N. & Quick, A. (1988) *Infertility Services: a Desperate Case*. GLAGHC, London.

Pfeffer, N. & Woollett, A. (1983) *The Experience of Infertility*. Virago, London.

Philipp, E. (1984) *Overcoming Childlessness: its Causes and What to do With Them*. Hamlyn, London.

Rajfer, J. (ed.) (1990) *Common Problems in Infertility and Impotence*. Year Book Medical Publishers Inc., Chicago.

Ragni, G. & Caccamo, A. (1992) Negative effect of stress of IVF program on quality of semen. *Acta Eur Fertil*, **23**, 21–23.

Rogers, C.R. (1951) *Client-Centred Therapy*. Houghton Mifflin, Boston.

Rosen, D. (1994) The Room. *Issue* (Summer), p.3.

Rubinstein, B.B. (1951) An emotional factor in infertility. *Fertil Steril*, **2**, 80.

Sandler, B. (1968) Emotional stress and infertility. *Journals of Psychosomatic Research*, **12**, 51–59.

Savage, M.O. (1992) Artificial donor insemination in Yaounde: some sociocultural considerations. *Soc Sci Med*, **35**, 907–913.

Schover, L.R., Collins, R.L. & Richards, S. (1992) Psychological aspects of donor insemination: evaluation and follow-up of recipient couples. *Fertil Steril*, **57**, 583–590.

Schover, L.R., Rothmann, S.A. & Collins, R.L. (1992) The personality and motivation of semen donors: a comparison with oocyte donors. *Human Reproduction*, **7**, 575–579.

Scutt, J.A. (ed.) (1990) *The Baby Machine*. Green Print, London.

Scutt, J.A. (1990) Women's bodies, patriarchal principles – Genetic and reproductive engineering and the law. In *The Baby Machine* (ed. J.A. Scutt), pp.185–234. Green Print, London.

Sharpe, R.M. & Skakkebaek, N.E. (1993) Are estrogens involved in falling sperm counts and disorders of the male reproductive tract. *The Lancet*, **341**, 1392–1395.

Sichel, M.P. (1991) Women and the gynaecologist. Difficulties in comprehension. *Clin Expt Obstet Gynecol.*, **18**, 57–59.

Silman, R. (ed.) (1993) *Virgin Birth*. WFT Press, London.

Singer, P. & Wells, D. (1984) *The Reproduction Revolution: New Ways of Making Babies*. Oxford University Press, Oxford, UK.

Snowden, R., Mitchell, G.D. & Snowden, E. (1983) *Artificial Reproduction: a Social Investigation*. George Allen & Unwin, London.

Snowden, R. & Snowden, E. (1993) *The Gift of a Child* (2nd ed.). Exeter University Press, Exeter.

Stanton, A.L. (1991) Cognitive appraisals, copying processes and adjustment to infertility. In *Infertility Perspectives from Stress and Coping Research* (eds. A.L. Stanton & C. Dunkel-Schetter), Plenum Press, New York.

Stone, B. (1990) Roman Catholic casuistry and the moral standing of the human embryo. In *The Status of the Human Embryo: Perspectives From Moral Tradition* (eds. G.R. Dunstan & M.J. Sellers), pp.74–85. King Edward's Hospital Fund for London.

Strathern, M. (1980) No nature, no culture: the Hagen case. In *Nature, Culture and Gender* (eds. C. MacCormack & M. Strathern), pp.174–222. Cambridge University Press, Cambridge.

Strathern, M. (1992) *Reproducing the Future*. Manchester University Press, Manchester.

Strathern, M. (1993) In *Virgin Birth* (ed. R. Silman), pp.20–29. WFT Press, London.

Timoney, A.G., Lee, S. & Shaw, J.R. (1990) Implantation of sperm reservoirs for ejaculatory failure in spinally injured males. *Journal of Urology*, **143**, Supplement, 389A.

Van Dyck, J. (1995) *Manufacturing Babies and Public Consent*. MacMillan, London.

Van Hoose, W.H. & Worth, M.R. (1982) *Adulthood in the Life Cycle*. William C. Brown, Dubuque.

Van Thiel, M., Mantadakis, E., Vekemans, M., Gillot, M. & de Vries, F. (1990) Etude, par entretiens et tests projectifs, du psychisme de patient(e)s avant recours a l'insemination artificielle par donneur anonyme. *J. Gynecol Obstet Biol Reprod* (Paris) 19, 823–828. (A Psychological study, using interviews and projective tests on patients seeking anonymous donor artificial insemination).

Vantress, C.E. (1986) Social and cultural foundations. In *An Introduction to the Counselling Profession* (eds. M.D. Lewis, R.L. Hayes & A. Lewis). FE Peacock, Itasca.

Warnock Report (1984) *Report of the Committee of Inquiry into Human Fertilisation and Embryology.* HMSO, London.

Wheeler, M. (1994) Mind over matter: can emotional blocks cause infertility: *Journal of Fertility Counselling*, **1**, 11–14.

World Health Organisation (1990) *Laboratory Manual for Semen Analysis.* Cambridge University Press, Cambridge.

Zavos, P.M. (1985) Seminal parameters of ejaculates collected from oligospermic and normospermic patients via masturbation and at intercourse with the use of a Silastic* seminal fluid collection device. *Fertil Steril*, **44**, 517–520.

Glossary

*Advanced embryo stage:*Any stage beyond 64-cell could be considered to be an advanced embryo. At this stage the embryo would be called an early blastocyst. It is at this point that an embryo may be viable to prepare for implantation.

Agglutination: Commonly occurs when antisperm antibodies are present in the semen. Sometimes, especially when the sperm count is very high, sperm may do this spontaneously, even when antibodies are not present.

AIDS and HIV: Antibodies for the human immunodeficiency virus (HIV) may be tested for. The presence of these indicates that the person is likely to develop acquired immune deficiency syndrome (AIDS) some time in the future.

Amplitude of head displacement (ALH): This is only quantifiable by the use of computer automated semen analysis (q.v.) (CASA). As sperm move they describe the pattern of a sine wave. The ALH is a measure of the distance from the peak to the trough of the waveform. It is believed that the ALH gives us information on sperm function. Too small an ALH demonstrates dysfunction as does too large a figure. The optimal ALH has not yet been defined.

Ampulla: The part of the fallopian tube which is close to the fimbrial opening, which is the end which is equipped to pick up the ovum/ova. The ampulla is the site of fertilisation. From here the embryo will travel down to the uterus, a journey which takes 5 to 8 days.

Antisperm antibodies: Everyone makes antibodies, but not usually against themselves. Some men, for reasons unknown begin to make antibodies to their own sperm. This usually produces agglutination of the sperm, which therefore interferes with fertility. When a man has had a vasectomy, which is then reversed, the presence of antibodies is almost guaranteed.

Arrest: Embryos sometimes stop dividing. When they do this, it is described as cleavage arrest. It is fairly common in IVF. Animal work has shown that whereas arrest is common in IVF, embryos in the fallopian tube and uterus undergo much less arrest.

Assisted reproduction/conception treatment (ART): Term used to describe all infertility treatments collectively.

Asthenozoospermia: A condition in the male where less than 40% of the sperm show motility. It is also sometimes used to describe poor movement (see also *Progression*).

Azoospermia: Condition where a man has no sperm in his ejaculate.

Biopsy-ICSI: is the same as ICSI, except that the sperm used are derived from testicular biopsy. Here a fine needle is inserted into the testes directly in order to extract sperm for injection.

Blighted ovum: A pseudopregnancy which occurs fairly commonly after IVF treatment. A pregnancy sac is present, which means hormone levels of oestrogen, progesterone and hCG will be high, but the sac does not contain a fetus. This type of pregnancy must be terminated by a dilatation and curettage. If not, there is a risk that the pregnancy might develop into a 'mole', a usually benign mass found growing in the uterus.

Borderline: Just outside the stated value for infertility.

Cervical insemination: When the semen sample or prepared sperm are placed around the cervix and not through it as with IUI. DI is often done this way, although, since the use of frozen–thawed samples became the norm we might get better results adopting IUI.

Cervix: The gateway to the uterus. It is found at the back of the vagina and provides a narrow opening (the os) which is usually filled with mucus. Sperm must negotiate the cervix and its mucus to reach the uterus.

Coital frequency: It is important when trying to conceive to have sex regularly. In the clinics this is often referred to as coital frequency. Poor coital frequency is often used as a euphemism for no sex, which obviously is highly disadvantageous.

Complete testicular failure: Results in azoospermia. May be confirmed by blood test (test for LH, FSH and testosterone) or by biopsy.

Counting chamber: These are used for carrying out sperm counts in semen analysis. The makes which are most usually encountered are:

- *Makler* The Rolls Royce of counting chambers.
- *Neubauer* Usually used for counting blood cells
- *Horwell* Value for money. Common amongst IVF units.

Computer automated semen analysis (CASA): Term used to describe semen analysis done by computer. Advantage is reproducibility. To date, human assessment is still as good as CASA, but machines and software are improving rapidly. CASA can give data for ALH and CVL which humans cannot. As data like ALH and CVL is better understood and is demonstrably able to predict sperm function, CASA will become more widely used and important.

Controlled studies: are the basis on which new treatments are tested in order to prove they are worthwhile options. These are research studies where a control group is established in parallel with the study group. The control group should match the study group with respect to age, type of infertility, duration of infertility etc., as closely as possible. The control group ideally would be 'treated' in a similar way to the study group, except that they would not receive whatever is being crucially tested.

Cryoprotectant: is added to semen so that it may be frozen. It contains special ingredients which help the sperm to survive freezing and thawing.

Cryptorchidism: A condition where one or both the testes have failed to migrate into the scrotal sac (hence the common description of 'undescended testes') can often result in azoospermia (even when the testes have been lowered by surgery or drugs), although in some cases function can be adequate.

Curvilinear velocity (CVL): may only be obtained through CASA. It is a measure of the speed that the sperm are swimming at. Note CVL is different from straight line velocity, which may also be computed through CASA.

Demonstrate efficacy: When controlled studies are done, the object is to demonstrate that whatever drug or surgical treatment on offer is 'effective', hence to demonstrate efficacy.

Diagnostic IVF cycle: IVF provides limited options for treatment of infertility. For tubal infertility in the female it is the treatment option of choice. For all other infertilities, IVF is not the only option. In many cases though, an early IVF attempt is useful as a means of determining whether fertilisation is possible. Thus it is useful as a means of confirming sperm function. Once this is established further IVF cycles should be placed in abeyance until other options have been explored and exhausted.

Direct oocyte transfer (DOT): is a procedure just like GIFT. It differs only in the site that the eggs and prepared sperm are placed immediately after egg recovery. The site of transfer is the womb.

Donor insemination (DI): Men with good semen analysis (but not necessarily proven function) donate semen samples for the use of couples infertile as a consequence of male infertility. The samples must be frozen and quarantined (during which tests for HIV are done) before use.

Donors: Screening for sexually transmitted disease, common bacterial, fungal and virus infections should all be done on a routine basis. Genetic screening is also a prerequisite. Age, physical characteristics, character, etc., may all be taken into consideration, but cut-off points will almost certainly differ from clinic to clinic, perhaps according to whether their bank is well filled or not.

Ectopic pregnancies: Pregnancies that establish themselves outside the uterus, usually in a fallopian tube, are called ectopic pregnancies. The patient must have the pregnancy dealt with; usually by removal of the tube where the fetus is growing. Residual function in a tube where an ectopic has been is usually poor.

Electroejaculation: Used for men with impotence or who are spinally injured, usually the semen obtained in this way will be prepared and used for IUI, GIFT or IVF. However, if there is some evidence of residual sperm function (i.e. swim up is just adequate or a few sperm are able to penetrate mucus), IUI, IVF or GIFT may be offered depending on the severity of dysfunction. The key to treatment lies in the quality of the preparation (the hunt for and isolation of elite sperm). In my opinion, if there is no obvious female factor, IVF and GIFT are still questionable treatment options for male factor.

Embryo transfer: Up to three embryos will be placed in the uterus transcervically, using a special catheter (similar to IUI). It is a non-surgical procedure which normally takes less than 10 minutes to complete.

Empirical options for men: Other empirical treatments may be of value, but these have not been proven in controlled studies. Tamoxifen, mesterolone, gonadotrophin injections, hCG and vitamin supplements may all be given to the male patient and are 'popular' supplementary therapies, especially with urologists. The tamoxifen is useful in cases where the blood levels of the sex hormones are normal. In these cases, tamoxifen (dose of 20 mg twice daily for 30–60 days) may raise the count significantly. Sperm quality is rarely improved, but you certainly get more of the same (useful perhaps if considering semen preparation and IUI). Mesterolone is usually only of value if the testosterone levels are below 15 nM. In these cases, motility is usually poor. A dose of 25 mg of Mesterolone on a daily basis for 60 days should then boost testosterone levels and the percentage motility. The use of gonadotrophins or hCG may be of benefit. Here the rationale is that they probably will not have any effect, but their use will not hurt. Courses of treatment are usually given for three months prior to assisted conception. Finally, more recently, methods have relied on medium supplements. Pentoxyfylline and taurine have been used to 'supercharge' sperm (possibly converting some of the poorer sperm into elite ones) during semen preparation, whilst some specialists also add vitamin E to the preparation media.

Empirical superovulation (ES): The simple rationale is, if there are more eggs, there might be a better chance of success. With ES, the female partner is given daily injections of gonadotrophins (drugs that promote multiple follicle development in the ovaries). The response of the ovaries is monitored regularly by ultrasound. When two to three mature follicles are seen, a final injection of human chorionic gonadotrophin (hCG) is given to produce ovulation. After this the couple are advised to have sex in the next 24 to 48 hours. If there are more than four mature follicles, hCG is withheld and the cycle is abandoned because the chances of a risky multiple pregnancy become too high (although multiple pregnancy in cases of male infertility are very rare).

Epididymis: Part of the testis, where the sperm mature and are stored prior to ejaculation.

Epididymal cysts: block the epididymis causing oligozoospermia or azoospermia by blocking the passage of sperm to the vas.

Erectile dysfunction: Term used to describe the situation when the penis is unable to become erect. Also called impotence.

Failure to fertilise in IVF: One of the most feared results during IVF. It means no embryos, no transfer and no chance of conception. It occurs 10–20% of the time, of which up to half may arise even when the semen analysis is normal.

Fallopian tube: The tube that picks up eggs via its open ending with fimbriae (specialised tissue that helps to catch the egg) and then transports them down its tube to the uterus. Fertilisation occurs in the ampulla of the tube. The developing early embryo then travels down the tube to the uterus.

Fertilisation: During fertilisation the sperm must penetrate the egg. Failure of penetration means that an embryo will not be created, hence nothing will be transferred and the IVF has failed.

Follicle stimulating hormone (FSH): acts on Sertoli cells which have an intimate relationship with sperm and testosterone (promotes sperm development) levels (Butt, 1982). Low LH or FSH levels indicate hypogonadic function, which might respond to tamoxifen, hCG or FSH therapy. High FSH levels are usually an indication of testicular failure. High testosterone may be an indication of testicular cancer and should be followed up by an urologist.

Frozen–thawed semen samples: Donor samples used for DI must be frozen–

thawed. Because our cryoprotectants and methods are not yet optimized, such samples seem to have reduced fertility, which is correctable by carrying out sperm preparation.

Human chorionic gonadotrophin (hCG): A hormone released during pregnancy. It has a very similar structure to LH, and the two may be substituted for each other. It is used routinely to produce ovulation in fertility treatments such as IVF.

Human Fertilisation and Embryology Authority (HFEA): is the body that regulates IVF, the freezing of semen and embryos and DI in the UK.

Hyperactivated: Sperm must go through a state where it seems to 'thresh' about wildly. Having undergone hyperactivation the sperm is then ready to penetrate an egg to fertilise it.

Hypogonadism: State where LH and or FSH levels in the blood are deficient.

Hypothalamus: The part of the brain that controls the pituitary.

Intracytoplasmic sperm injection (ICSI): ICSI is carried out when the sperm count or motility is very poor. Sperm may be picked up using a very fine needle and injected into the egg direct. The injected egg is then subjected to IVF.

Ideopathic: Unexplained.

Image analysis: CASA relies on software which is based on image analysis.

Liquid nitrogen: Used to freeze and store semen and embryos.

Luteinising hormone (LH): Produces ovulation in women, and is also called interstitial cell stimulating hormone in men where it acts on the testes as a secondary hormone influencing testosterone production (see also *Follicle stimulating hormone* (FSH)).

Microepididymal sperm aspiration (MESA): Allows sperm to be obtained from azoospermic men, with vasal absence or blockage. This procedure requires surgery. A fine needle may be inserted into the epididymis allowing some motile sperm to be extracted. This sperm is then prepared and used for IVF or for microinjection into ova as per ICSI.

Mid cycle: Is the term used to describe the part of the female cycle where we expect ovulation to occur.

Miscarriage: Occurs regularly during fertility treatments. Up to one in four of the pregnancies established will not produce a live birth, as they will end spontaneously.

Mucus: Secretion found in the cervix. Good mucus is highly receptive to good active sperm. The best sperm are able to penetrate mucus to arrive in the uterus; thus good mucus provides a useful means of assessing sperm function.

Oligoasthenoteratozoospermia: Term used to describe oligoasthenozoospermia combined with teratozoospermia (q.v.).

Oligoasthenozoospermia: Term describing oligozoospermia combined with asthenozoospermia (q.v.).

Oligozoospermia: Term describing poor sperm count (less than 20 million per ml).

Ovum/Ova: An immature egg is called an oocyte. A mature egg is called an ovum, a number of mature eggs are called ova.

Ovarian stimulation: This is done when the ovary is not working properly. When the female cycle is absent (anovulation) or sporadic (oligomenorrhœa), this will be done to get the ovary 'on-line' again. For AC/ART when we wish to get more eggs we superovulate, which is ovarian stimulation, but with stronger drugs or a higher dose.

Ovum collection: For DOT, GIFT and IVF we need to collect the eggs before we can select and transfer them back to the patient. Thus we need to carry out ovum collection to recover the eggs. This used to be done laparoscopically, but is now done using ultrasound (either abdominally or vaginally).

Papaverine injections: an injectable drug which produces an erection in the penis. Can cause problems when the erection will not subside, which then needs surgical draining.

Penile prostheses: Surgically inserted devices to help overcome impotence. Especially useful in cases of non-psychogenic impotence, such as spinal injury cases.

Pituitary: The gland just beneath the brain which makes, stores and releases a range of hormones, particularly luteinising hormone and follicle stimulating hormone (q.v.), which control ovulation and spermatogenesis.

Plastic straws: Semen samples and spare embryos derived from IVF are frozen and stored in specially manufactured plastic straws.

Polyspermy: (see *Triploid embryos*) When more than one sperm enters the egg we have polyspermy. Such eggs are not viable.

Poor fertilisation rates: A man with a normal semen analysis may still produce poor fertilisation rates. This might be due to antisperm antibody presence or indeed to poor function. Poor fertilisation rates suggest poor sperm function. Persistently poor fertilisation rates may be an indication that donor sperm might be needed. If so, and the female partner has no obvious infertility, DI should be the next option rather than DIVF. One diagnostic DIVF cycle might be carried out, but if fertilisation rates are good, DI would then be the preferred option for at least 6 to 12 further attempts.

Post coital test (PCT): is also useful provided its timing is done well. The time of ovulation is best determined by serial ultrasound scanning. The PCT is performed 6 to 10 hours post coitus. Mucus from both the internal os and the low cervix is examined. The test is positive if 10 motile sperm per high power field are observed ($\times$ 40 objective). It is important to determine how well the sperm survive in the mucus.

Prednisone: Steroid sometimes used for treating antisperm antibodies, which can have serious risks and complications.

Pregnancy rates: There are many ways of describing a clinic's success rate. For instance, the most honest way is to describe the live birth rate per treatment cycle (the national average for IVF without donor sperm is 9%). Note that even this figure may be distorted if we count twins as two live births and triplets as three. So in a way we should be quoting deliveries per cycle where multiple births still count as one delivery. Some units quote pregnancy rate and not live births/delivery rates. Since about one in four pregnancies are lost during AC/ART our 9% live birth rate would translate to ~ 13% pregnancy rate. Some clinics quote pregnancy rate per embryo transfer. In an average clinic 10% of cycles will not achieve an embryo transfer, thus boosting the success rate to ~15% per embryo transfer. Thus it is important to listen carefully when success rates are reported. It is always worthwhile asking specifically what the live birth rate per *cycle* is.

Progression: is the word used to describe the forward mobility of sperm in a semen sample. It is a subjective method, which takes into account not just the speed with which the sperm move, but also whether they move with purpose or not (i.e. if they chase their own tail they will be scored poorly).

Pronuclei The pronunclei are visible in the fertilised egg, some 16 to 24 hours after the sperm has first penetrated the egg. Usually, only two pronuclei are visible, one deriving from the ovum and one from the sperm. In polyspermic fertilization three or four pronuclei might be seen.

Psychogenic impotence: Impotence arising from stress and anxiety rather than from a physical disorder, such as a spinal injury or a neurological problem.

Risks and complications: All treatment options carry risks and known complications. Laparascopy necessitates the use of general anaesthesia. Anaesthetic complications can sometimes result in death. Laparoscopy itself may result in a perforated bowel. ART may sometimes produce hyperstimulation syndrome in the female patient, when the ovaries become enlarged and the abdomen full of fluid. All treatments carry some form of risk and the possibility of complications.

Semen analysis: Not a reliable method for diagnosis of male infertility. Semen analysis tells us whether sperm are present or not in the semen sample. In traditional analysis we will obtain information on how many sperm are present and what percentage are moving. In IVF clinics we will also get an accurate assessment of the percentage of sperm which have an abnormal appearance.

Semen preparation: Almost all AC/ART relies on preparing the sperm, which depends on the migratory properties of the functional sperm. Most methods involve the use of a centrifuge.

Sensate focus: This is a set of exercises popularised by Masters and Johnson, involving a predetermined set of exercises which clients agree to undergo according to a prescribed pattern. It is particularly useful in cases of impotence, as well as for other types of sexual dysfunction. In brief, sensate focus involves a ban on full penetrative sex at the start. The client is encouraged to focus on exploring the sensations of feeling and touching.

To begin with, certain parts of the body will be placed off-limits, but as the exercises progress, the couple are allowed to move on to other exercises, until finally full sex is allowed to take place.

Severe male infertility: Where the motile sperm count is less than 4 million sperm per ml, we are probably safe in diagnosing severe male infertility. Usually we are dealing with oligoasthenozoospermia and DI is also usually a reasonable option.

Severe spinal injuries: Arise as a consequence of motor accidents, diving into swimming pools and other activities which may produce serious trauma to the neck and spine when accidents occur. Usually a patient with spinal injury will be wheelchair bound. The severity of the injury will determine whether the injured person has use of his upper body.

Sex therapy: Commonly referred to when talking about impotence. Also relevant in cases involving deviant sexual behaviour, e.g. transvestitism, fetishes etc. Best known advocates are Masters and Johnson.

Sperm function: Semen analysis reveals little about sperm function. A functional sperm is one that will fertilise an egg. IVF is therefore a useful diagnostic test.

Sperm–mucus contact test (SMCT): Provides sufficient data for accurate diagnosis of sperm function or dysfunction. Ideally, for standardisation and to control against poor mucus quality, donor mucus and semen should be obtainable in large amounts so that cross checks may also be carried out.

Spermatoceles: Implants which are attached to the *vas deferens* and used to act as sperm reservoirs. These devices may then be aspirated by means of a needle and syringe. The aspirated sperms may then be prepared and used for treatment.

Spermatogenesis: Process describing the meiotic production of germ cells occurring in the testis (see also under *Testes*).

Spermiogenesis: Once sperm have completed meiosis, they still need time to mature. Immature sperm are still round cells. The process for a round cell which has completed meiosis to become a mature motile sperm is called spermiogenesis (see also under *Testes*).

Sub-optimal semen analysis: A semen analysis revealing oligozoospermia, asthenozoospermia or teratozoospermia would be described as sub-optimal. Oligoasthenozoospermia is worse than sub-optimal.

Superovulation: The use of injectable purified human hormones (luteinising hormone and follicle stimulating hormone (qv) or the latter alone) which stimulate the ovaries to produce between 2 and 10 follicles, hence reasonably large numbers of ova to use in IUI, GIFT or IVF.

Teratozoospermia: Male infertility when count and motility are okay but the sperm have an abnormal morphology. In other words the sperm look 'ugly' and so are less likely to be able to fertilise an egg (more than 60% abnormal morphology is bad).

Testes: Site of spermatogenesis. A man has two testes. One working testis is usually enough. The testes are reproductive organs in the body, which on a minute to minute basis are actively involved in mitosis and meiosis (cell division). Sperm start their life as round cells called spermatogonia. These undergo mitosis (normal cell division) until they begin meiosis (cell division which only reproductive cells such as sperm and ova undergo, resulting in each cell having only 23 chromosomes instead of the normal 46). The first stage of meiosis involves primary spermatocytes and secondary spermatocytes. The secondary spermatocytes must still undergo a final process during which they pass through a stage when they become spermatids (early spermatids are still round cells and it is only during the final period as a spermatid that the characteristic 'tadpole' shape of adult sperm becomes apparent. From spermatogonia to mature sperm takes 60–70 days.

Testicular biopsy: A needle is placed into the testis to draw out tissue which may then be examined to determine whether the testis is still making sperm or not.

Testosterone: Male hormone with corresponding actions in males to that of oestrogen in females.

Timing of insemination: It is important to get the timing of insemination right. Indeed the timing of sex, ovum collection etc., must all be carefully determined. Timing is manipulated by administering hCG (q.v.) and also monitored by the use of ultrasound. The size of the follicle helps specialists to determine the maturity of the follicle. Sometimes blood hormone levels are also used to monitor and determine timing of procedures.

Triploid embryos: An egg which has been fertilised by two sperm or a defective ovum which has been fertilised by one sperm. Double sperm entry is the most common cause and occurs in up to 5% of all fertilisations in IVF.

Twins and triplets: A multiple pregnancy. Common end result of successful assisted conception treatment.

Uterus: The womb. This is where the embryo may implant, thereby establishing a pregnancy.

Volume of semen: Normal volume ranges from 1 to 10 ml. Natural pregnancies may occur with as little as 0.5 ml. Pregnancies with IUI, GIFT or IVF may be achieved with as little as 0.1 ml.

Varicocoele: Condition where the spermatic vein, usually on the left side, is enlarged, resulting in increased blood flow to the scrotum, which is thought to raise the temperature of the scrotum from 34°C to 37°C, thereby supposedly causing spermatogenic disruption until, in theory, the varicocoele is dealt with, surgical intervention may be considered, but even here success rates vary from nil to 25%.

Vas deferens: Tube connecting the epididymis, where sperm are stored to the urethra.

Vasectomy: The vas deferens is cut and tied off. This induces infertility and is a common method of birth control for men who decide that they do not want any further children. There are rather too many incidences of vasectomy reversal, indicating perhaps too ready a will to offer or to accept surgery without sufficient prior thought.

Vasogram: X-ray test using radio-opaque dye which allows tubal patency of the *vas deferens* to be checked (similar to HSG).

Yohimbine: A drug which is occasionally used for treating impotence. It is not licensed for this use so specialists in the UK do not normally prescribe it.

Index